The origins of
Somerset

general editor
Nick Higham

already published in the series
The origins of Lancashire   *Denise Kenyon*

The origins of
Somerset

Michael Costen

Manchester University Press
Manchester and New York

Distributed exclusively in the USA and Canada by St. Martin's Press

Published by Manchester University Press
Oxford Road, Manchester M13 9PL, UK
and Room 400, 175 Fifth Avenue, New York, NY 10010, USA

Distributed exclusively in the USA and Canada
by St. Martin's Press, Inc., 175 Fifth Avenue, New York,
NY 10010, USA

A catalogue record for this book is available from the British Library

Library of Congress cataloging in publication data
Costen, M. D.
    The origins of Somerset / Michael Costen.
        p.   cm.—(origins of the Shire)
    Includes bibliographical references and index.
    ISBN 0-7190-3399-3 (hardback).—ISBN 0-7190-3675-5 (paperback)
    1. Somerset (England)—History.   2. Anglo-Saxons—England—
Somerset.   3. Britons—England—Somerset.   4. Romans—England—
Somerset.   I. Title.   II. Series.
DA670.S5C75   1992
942.3'801—dc20   91-33531

ISBN   0 7190 3399-3 *hardback*
       0 7190 3675-5 *paperback*

Phototypeset in Hong Kong by Best-set Typesetter Limited
Printed in Great Britain by Bell and Bain Ltd, Glasgow

Contents

Figures and plates

Figures

Plates

Abbreviations

ASC	Whitelock, D., Douglas, D. C. and Tucker, S. I. (eds and trans.) *The Anglo-Saxon Chronicle*: A Revised Translation (London, 1965)
BAR	British Archaeological Reports, Oxford
DB	Thorn, C. and Thorn F. (eds and trans.) *The Domesday Book: Somerset* (Chichester, 1980)
D & C, Wells	*Calendar of the Manuscripts of the Dean and Chapter of Wells*, Historical Manuscripts Commission, vols I & II (London, 1907 and 1914)
EHR	*English Historical Review*
OE	Old English
OW	Old Welsh
PDAES	*Proceedings of the Devon Archaeological Exploration Society*
PSANHS	*Proceedings of the Somerset Archaeological and Natural History Society*
S & DN & Q	*Somerset and Dorset Notes and Queries*
S.	Sawyer, P., *Anglo-Saxon Charters; An Annotated List and Bibliography* (London, 1968)
SRS	Somerset Record Society
TRHS	*Transactions of the Royal Historical Society*
VCH	Page, W. (ed.), vols I & II (London, 1906 and 1911) and Dunning, R. W. (ed.), vols III, IV & V (London, 1974, 1978 and 1985), *A History of the County of Somerset*

Manuscript sources

BL 15350	British Library Additional Manuscript 15350, the chartulary of Winchester Cathedral
D/D/Ca. 300	Deposition Book in Somerset County Record Office
D/D/Rt 118	The Tithe award and Map for West Camel parish, 1842 in Somerset County Record Office, Taunton
D/D/Rt 143	The tithe award and map for Ditcheat parish, 1840 in Somerset County Record Office, Taunton
D/D/Rt 277	The Tithe Map and Award for Carhampton, 1840
D/D/Rt 6	The Tithe award and map for Staplegrove parish, dated 1837, in the Somerset Record Office, Taunton
DD/SE Box 3	A survey of the bounds of Clifton Parish, 1580, Somerset Record Office, Taunton
Egerton 3321	British Library, Egerton MS 3321, Extent of the lands of the Abbey of Glastonbury, 1327
Liber Albus	Vols I & II in the library of Wells Cathedral, two manuscript volumes of charters, deeds, leases, surveys and minutes
R.5.33	Trinity College Cambridge, MS Surveys of the lands of Glastonbury Abbey of the twelfth and early thirteenth centuries
T/Ph/VCH 5(i)	copy in Somerset Record Office of Ministers ✓ Accounts at Lambeth Palace

Acknowledgements

I am grateful to Dr C. Gerrard and Dr R. H. Leech for per-mission to make use of material in their unpublished theses and to Dr Nicholas Higham for allowing me access to several articles which were still in press when this book was written. Much work in the Somerset County Record Office over the years has been made easier and more pleasant by the help of many friends who are members of the staff. Mr Robin Bush, Deputy County Archivist and Miss Susan Berry have been particularly kind as has Mr Stephen Hobbs, now County Archivist in Wiltshire. Mr David Bromwich, County Local History Librarian and Dr Steve Minnit of the Somerset County Museum have always been helpful. I also owe a profound debt of gratitude to several colleagues at the University of Bristol. Mick Aston, Reader in Archaeology, has been an especial help and I have benefited from many talks with him as well as much practical help. Dr Joe Bettey has been very kind in offering advice and criticism and Dr Peter Hardy helped me with the geology of the county. Mrs Ruth Hill has shouldered much routine and protected me from the telephone so that I could work. Dr Nicholas Higham has saved me from several errors, but has not imposed his views upon me, so that any misinterpretations are my own. Over the years I have benefited from discussing much of the material in this book with the adult students in my classes and one-day conferences; I owe them a debt of gratitude which may surprise some of them, but which is nevertheless real.

General Editor's preface

The shire was the most important single unit of government, justice and social organisation throughout the Later Middle Ages and on into the Modern period. An understanding of the shire is, therefore, fundamental to English history of all sorts and of all periods – be it conducted on a national, regional or local basis.

This series sets out to explore the origins of each shire in the Early Middle Ages. Archaeological evidence for settlement hierarchies and social territories in later prehistory and the Roman period is necessarily the starting point. The shire and its component parts are then explored in detail during the Anglo-Saxon period. A series of leading scholars with a particular regional expertise have brought together evidence drawn from literary and documentary sources, place-name research and archaeological fieldwork to present a stimulating picture of the territorial history of the English shires, and the parishes, estates and hundreds of which they were formed.

In some instances the results stress the degree of continuity across periods as long as a millennium. Elsewhere, these studies underline the arbitrary nature of the shire and the intentional break with the past, particularly where the West Saxon King, Edward the Elder, imposed his southern ideas concerning local organisation on the regional communities of the English Midlands.

These volumes will each be a great asset to historians and all those interested in their own localities, offering an open door into a period of the past which has, up to now, for many, been too difficult or obscure to attempt an entry.

Nick Higham

Introduction

This is a history, and as such suffers from all the faults of sub-jectivity which mark it out as the view of one person. It covers a period in the early history of Somerset when documentary material is non-existent or at best very sparse and so it relies on archaeological sources and studies such as place-names, as well as upon charters and documentary sources such as the Anglo-Saxon Chronicle and the Domesday Book. Much of this book is, therefore, speculative. Nevertheless it seems a worthwhile exercise to try to outline a possible history for the county up to about 1150. I have stopped at that point because I believe that 'Somerset', essentially as we see it today, once we take away the modern trappings of technical change, had been formed by that date. The historic county was in existence. Its local com-munities had taken on the shape thay have today. Most of the towns were there. The backbone of its communications existed. The foundations of local administration had been laid. The church had assumed the organisation and coverage of the com-munity which it has retained to this day, even if the monasteries have gone. Both the idea and the substance of Somerset are recognisable.

Underlying the book are two themes. The first is that the county, even before it can be recognised as such, has been shaped by its rulers, whether they were Iron Age chieftains, Romano-British aristocrats or Anglo-Saxon thegns. The economic and cultural needs of these people determined the way in which estates were organised and influenced the development of the countryside in all its diversity. It is to these people that we owe the fundemental 'shape' of the county. By that I mean not only its boundaries, but also its landscape; the way in which it was divided up; the placing of roads, towns, churches; the patterns of farming; the existence of villages and farms; society and social relationships. The second theme is that of the ordinary people, who endured. The neolithic men and women were the ancestors of the men and women of the Norman countryside. Because we know so little about individuals prior to early modern times the history of the community of Somerset must neccessarily be told through the physical world they inhabited. They shaped it and it shaped them.

Most modern scholarship which is concerned with the period up to the High Middle Ages consists either of monographs which concentrate on a particular topic or place – the excavation of a site, the study of a single town, or they follow a theme which covers the whole country. I have tried to draw together much of that endeavour and apply it to Somerset. In this way I hope that the county will be seen in context, as part of the history of a larger and more diverse whole, yet having about it the uniqueness that it undoubtedly has. Everyone with eyes to see knows that Devon and Somerset are different one from another and that Wiltshire is different again. I hope I shall have explained why that is so.

1

The earliest farmers

The county of Somerset offers strong contrasts of geography and geology, stretching as it does across Exmoor in the west, the Levels in the centre and out to the hills around Bath in the north-east. The county can be divided into five regions.

In the west of the county is the high ground of Exmoor, rising to 519 metres at Dunkery Beacon. Exmoor and the Brendons, together with the Quantocks, are chiefly composed of Devonian rocks, slates and sandstones with some limestones. The whole area has a high rainfall and the soils often drain badly, leaving them acid. Here the moors were substantially unenclosed until recent times and the landscape today consists of a mixture of open moorland and large enclosed pastures, with woodlands on the more sheltered slopes. Although the land drops northward towards the sea, the north coast has imposing cliffs, often heavily wooded. To the east the moor merges into the Brendon Hills, which have a generally east-west alignment, and which drop away south to the hilly confused landscape of Devon north of Tiverton. Yet further east lie the Quantock Hills, which rise in places to over 300 metres. These hills run north-west to south-east and are divided from the Brendons by the valley of the Doniford Stream. The hills are surrounded by Permian and Triassic rocks which give pebble conglomerates in the west and around Taunton the red Triassic mudstone which gives the farm-lands of the district their red soil. The whole area is enclosed by the rivers Tone and Parrett, which make a natural boundary between highland and lowland Somerset. However, the boundary on the south and west, with Devon, is quite arbitrary.

The centre of the county is occupied by the river valleys of the Axe, Brue, Cary, Yeo and Parrett rivers. In the Jurassic period the whole area which is now lowland Somerset was submerged by a sea and the lower Liassic mud of the Levels survives here, with recent deposits of peat covering large areas. This land is generally lowlying and the rivers are slow moving as they cross the flat plains. Today many of them have artificially raised banks in their lower courses, since the combination of land which is often only a few metres above mean sea level, rivers which bring water to the sea from much higher ground, and the extraordinary range of tides in the Bristol Channel (over 13 metres during spring tides at Portishead), means that the rivers need careful management if the lands are not to suffer regular inundation. The Levels form the lowlying heartland of the county, broken by low hills, which rarely reach much over 100 metres, and by other blocks of higher ground, which form islands in the marshes.

The eastern and southern border of the county is characterised by fertile lands which are hilly but do not rise to great heights. Here Oxford clays and Fullers Earth run in bands from north to south. The most easterly part of the county is marked by a Greensand escarpment in the Selwood Forest. From the district around Yeovil southward this Cretaceous band spreads out and then turns westward in the Blackdown Hills.

To the North the Mendip Hills cross the county from the sea near Weston-super-Mare to the county boundary near Frome in the east. They are mostly composed of folded Carboniferous rocks, with Devonian cores to the anticlines. The Carboniferous rocks also form the Failand ridge, behind Clevedon and Portishead. They generally present steep slopes on both the north and south sides. At their highest point the Mendips reach 325 metres at Beacon Batch, near Burrington, but are characterised by an area of plateau where the land is usually over 250 metres high.

The final region is the coastal plain, which is divided by the Mendips into two. To the south of the Mendips the narrow coastal clay belt north of the river Parrett, provides some protection for the lower ground of the Levels to the east. On the

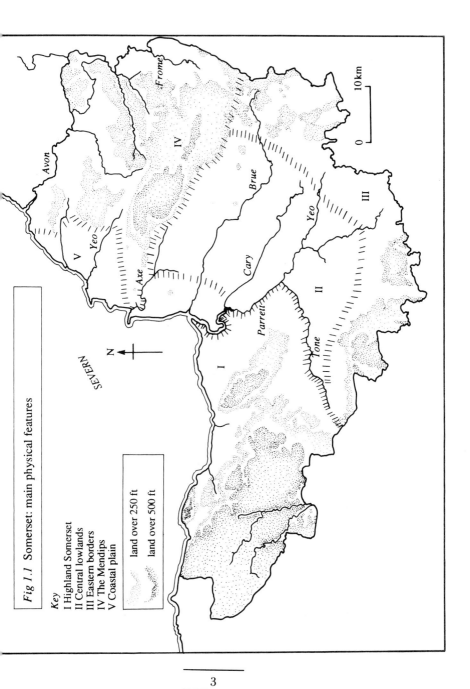

Fig 1.1 Somerset: main physical features

Key
I Highland Somerset
II Central lowlands
III Eastern borders
IV The Mendips
V Coastal plain

land over 250 ft
land over 500 ft

SEVERN

N

Avon
Frome
Yeo
Axe
Brue
Cary
Yeo
Parrett
Tone

0   10 km

northern side of the Mendips the basin of the Congresbury Yeo and the Kenn River produces another area of flat claylands, now dissected by drainage ditches (Fig. 1.1).

The first farmers

Agriculture began in Somerset with the advent of the Neolithic farmers who colonised the central region, in the Levels. At this time, *c.* 3900 BC, the Levels were reed swamp and into this wilderness these first farmers began to penetrate, building the wooden walkways which have survived, preserved in the peat, to enable them to cross the bogs (B. & J. Coles 1989, p. 156). The construction of these tracks shows that they were clearly made for people, rather than to allow the transport of animals, since they were too narrow to be used by cattle. The oldest of these constructions is the Sweet Track (Fig. 1.2). Evidence from its building suggests that the community which constructed it was well organised and settled and that the need to reach and use islands in the bogs was sufficiently pressing to push the farmers into the immense communal activity represented by the building of the track. The size of the undertaking, a wooden walkway some two kilometres in length, also attests to the size and commitment of the community, which carried through the operation using stone tools, in which trees were felled and split into planks. Rails of hazel, alder, ash, elm and holly were laid on the bog, pegs of the same materials were driven into the bog to stabilise the rails and peat piled on this surface to form a base for the planks which were then pegged into place (Coles 1982, p. 31). The builders selected their trees for planks and carried through the building campaign in a short period (Morgan 1977, p. 67; Coles and Orme 1984, p. 12), stockpiling the timber and then constructing the road in one campaign, presumably at a time when the waters of the marsh were at their lowest, towards the end of a dry summer. Recent evidence from dendrochronology dates the track securely to the years 3807–8 BC and shows that most of the timber was cut at the same time (Hillam *et al.* 1990, pp. 210–20). The track demonstrates skilled woodworking, implying some differentiation of occupation among the builders. Timber used in the walkway had come from two different sites, one at each end. The northern site was characterised by large mature oak trees, 400 years old, suggesting that permanent settlement on the islands was new, since the trees represent a natural woodland. The timber at the southern end had come from trees which were all about 120 years old, suggesting that the woodland had been cut down and then allowed to regrow (B. & J. Coles 1989, p. 156). Controlled felling was probably established here even at this early date. Here settlement may have been older, or the people who built the track may have been using a site which had already been occupied. Probably the settlement at Shapwick was already well established. However, their track was in use for only about ten years before it was overwhelmed by the growing peat bog. The variety of objects dropped along its course, pottery, wooden implements, flint arrow heads and even a jadeite axe from the Alps suggests that during the ten years 3807–3797 BC the track was regularly used in everyday domestic occupation as part of the farming life of the community (Hillam *et al.* 1990, note 4).

As the centuries passed the bogs became slightly drier and by *c.* 3600 BC fen woodland of alder and birch predominated, giving way once more to a new phase of flooding and the growth of raised bog before *c.* 3000 BC. As the landscape became wetter, tracks were again needed to link the islands of the Levels to the Polden hills and Wedmore island. The complex of tracks which linked Westhay, Honeygore and Burtle are dated *c.* 3500 BC and they represent a response to this need. By this time the farmers of the Levels were exploiting their woodlands systematically, coppicing their trees and using leaves for animal fodder, suggesting substantial populations, both of people and animals (Rackham 1977, pp. 65–71). There were four or five small settlements in the district on the islands and also on the Poldens between *c.* 3600 BC and 2900 BC (Coles 1989). The pollen records indicate that the landscape was increasingly open as trees were cleared. Grassland was important, suggesting a pastoral economy, but the farmers also grew some cereals (Hibbert 1978). Tracks continued to be built in the marshes right down into the Iron Age. Throughout an immensely long period from the Neolithic down to the present time the marshes have been occupied and exploited. Undoubtedly the tracks provided a way

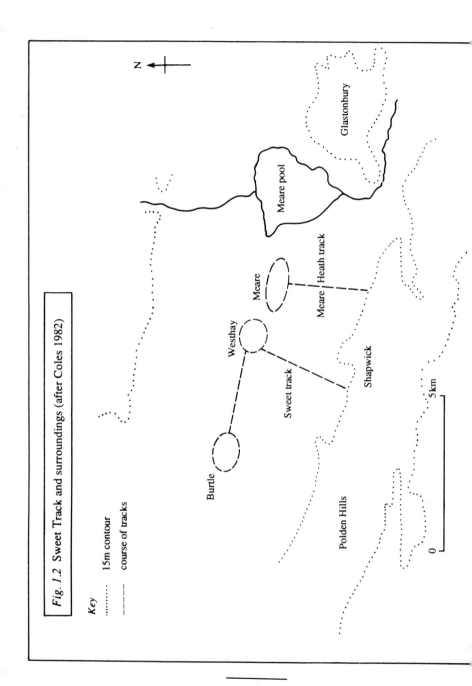

Fig. 1.2 Sweet Track and surroundings (after Coles 1982)

Key
.... 15m contour
———— course of tracks

Glastonbury

Meare pool

Meare

Meare Heath track

Westhay

Sweet track

Shapwick

Burtle

Polden Hills

0

5km

N

for the dwellers to cross from one island to another, but their very presence in the area shows that the marshes were not regarded as being a barren and inhospitable region; on the contrary, they offered special advantages to the early settlers. At the beginning of settlement the marshes were still reed swamp and in that condition probably offered fish in abundance as well as wild fowl. Some of the islands also provided opportunities for agriculture, the Burtles in particular being sandy and easy to cultivate.

There is also increasing evidence to suggest that other parts of the Levels outside the Brue valley were heavily used throughout the Neolithic period and onwards, although the lack of extensive peat deposits on King's Sedgemoor and elsewhere in the Levels has made the survival of evidence much more sparse (Coles 1989). These lowlying areas presented especially favourable conditions for settlement during this long early phase of agriculture. The extent of settlement in wetlands from Neolithic to Iron Age, both in Britain and in Continental Europe confirms that the farmers of the Somerset Levels were not unorthodox in their behaviour. Indeed it looks as if such sites were sought after rather than being marginal (Coles and Coles 1989).

To the north on the Mendips and in the hilly countryside between the Mendips and the Avon valley there is some slight evidence of settlement at the beginning of the Neolithic period (Fig. 1.3). At Chew Park, Rahtz and Greenfield found evidence of a small dwelling (Rahtz and Greenfield 1977), while pits at Ben Bridge (Rahtz and Greenfield 1977), Wells Cathedral (Minnit 1982) and Cadbury Castle (Alcock 1972, pp. 26–7, 108), also suggest permanent settlement. Pottery and signs of flint tool making at this site also suggest permanent occupation. Caves and rock shelters on the Mendips have produced sherds of vessels and flint implements (Balch 1926; 1928), but it is clear that settlement sites either still wait to be discovered, or have been destroyed by nature or subsequent human activity. Far too much has been found all over the region for settlement to have been very sparse, or concentrated only at the sites already mentioned.

At Cadbury Castle Neolithic pottery was discovered of a type well known in the South-West of England, similar to that found at Windmill Hill in Wiltshire, Maiden Castle in Dorset and

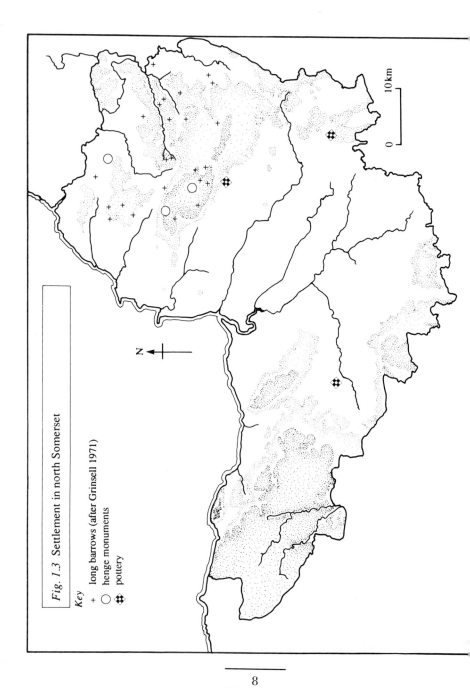

Fig. 1.3 Settlement in north Somerset

Key
+ long barrows (after Grinsell 1971)
○ henge monuments
✻ pottery

10 km

N

Hembury in Devon. Although the evidence is fragmentary, it is possible that settlement of some sort existed here *c.* 3300 BC (Alcock 1972, pp. 26–7). Nomads were hardly likely to have moved heavy pottery around with them, in any quantity, so the site was probably permanent. At Norton Fitzwarren, near Taunton, similar pottery and also flint tools have been discovered. This was a site which was later to become an important Bronze Age hillfort site (Langmaid 1971).

Stone and flint axes make up one of the largest bodies of finds from the Neolithic period. They have been found almost everywhere in the county, though the main concentration appears to be in the north of the county. The stone axes seem to come from a variety of sources with a majority made in Cornwall. The flint for the axes certainly came from outside the county. However, the chalk is very close in Wiltshire and would have been quite easily obtainable (Minnit 1982).

Social structure

Only in the north do we find ritual monuments. The chambered long barrows of northern Somerset were in use between *c.* 2800 BC and 1700 BC. They are part of the Severn-Cotswold group of long barrows and mark their most south-westerly limit (Grinsell 1971). These monuments were probably built between 2800 and 2400 BC (Darvill 1987a). In the same region the stone circles at Stanton Drew and the circular henge monuments at Priddy Circles and at Gorsey Bigbury, near Cheddar, are also part of the ritual activity of the same group of people, but date from several centuries later, between 2400 and 2100 BC (Darvill 1987a) (see Fig. 1.3).

Renfrew has suggested that the existence and spatial distribution of such monuments can be used to infer something of the organisation of the societies which constructed them. He suggests a hierarchy of monument types, long barrows, causewayed enclosures and henge monuments which can be grouped in both space and time to project a society which was hierarchically arranged and in which the development of larger and larger areas of political influence can be inferred from the growing scale of ritual monuments and their concentration in a few localities (Renfrew 1984). Thus long barrows represent an early stage of the accumulation of power, as the ritual centres for fairly small territorial groupings. Since they would only take *c.* 5,000 man-hours to construct the numbers of people available to work on them need not have been large. The barrows themselves would clearly be burial sites reserved only for the most important members of the society, showing that social differentiation existed. Cursus monuments represent a larger grouping, with the henge monuments denoting a yet larger scale of social cohesion. Renfrew's model is for Wessex and chiefly represents the chalklands of Wiltshire, Hampshire and Dorset, but it provides a model for the Mendip area, which suggests local groupings, with Whitesheet camp in Wiltshire as the relevant causewayed enclosure (Renfrew 1984, p. 236). Later, with the appearance of henge monuments, the area of the Mendips is well enough supplied to suggest that it was a unit in its own right, rather than a region peripheral to the western part of Salisbury Plain.

Even if this model supplies a satisfactory explanation for the observed monuments in the north of the county, we still know nothing about how or whether the men of the Levels and other parts of the county related to this group. It seems unlikely that they could have survived as a non-hierarchical grouping in an heroic society dominated by chieftains, especially as they too enjoyed the products of the specialist workers who produced tools and pottery, and who were probably under the control of the leaders of hierarchical groupings. Such a society was redistributive and control of such producers and products was an essential part of power. There are indications of serious and endemic warfare in other parts of the South-West, leading to the building of hilltop fortifications and it seems unlikely that Somerset escaped such activity (Mercer 1985).

In the mid-third millenium BC the major changes which are associated with the collapse of the belief systems which had produced the long barrows were also connected with an apparent decline in population and a change towards less intensive agriculture. Gradually the round barrows appeared as indicators of a new religious and social grouping, for which the henge monuments formed the superior ritual focus (Darvill 1987b, pp. 75–6).

Metalworking and hillforts

The introduction of metalworking into the societies of the South-West was a gradual process, not part of a catastrophic social upheaval, since the great monuments of the Neolithic period continued to be used into the early Bronze Age (*c.* 2000–1400 BC) (Ellison 1982, p. 45). Two barrows, Green Barrow at Priddy and the Camerton Barrow, have produced bronze daggers – ogival and grooved, and grooved – together with a bulb-headed decorated bronze pin at Camerton, which has parallels with material from Early Bronze Age Switzerland and Germany. These burials are part of Burgess's 'second category' graves of the Early Bronze Age, Wessex culture, and are the graves of a dominant warrior elite which had recently come from Brittany and had brought with it new religious ideas (Burgess 1974, p. 184). They built upon a rich indigenous culture which proved a powerful economic base for their activities. North-east Somerset was at the edge of the area of influence of this group who clearly took over from the Cotswold culture. The hoard from Milverton is also of this period, though part of the Arreton Tradition, rather than the Camerton-Snowshill type from the northern barrows (Minnit 1974).

By *c.* 1400 the Wessex aristocracy had disappeared and with them went the use of the henge monuments. Society underwent a profound change in its beliefs. The Middle Bronze Age (*c.* 1400–1000 BC) is remarkable for the quantity of bronze implements and ornaments which have been found. Fifteen hoards from the county form the basis of the 'Taunton' phase of metalworking the products of which spread into neighbouring Dorset and Wiltshire. Interestingly, the pottery associated with the metal finds is not all of one type. In the east, Deverill-Rimbury pottery occurs at Nettlebridge, Tynings Farm and Chard, while elsewhere the pottery of the Treviskar series from the South-West is common, suggesting that metalwork products were widely traded or exchanged across tribal groupings whose boundary lay somewhere on the north-eastern side of the Taunton Vale.

The society which produced this metalwork and used the pottery was sophisticated in its organisation. It was based upon a subsistence economy of mixed farming, with small settlements surrounded by arable fields. The extended family groups which occupied these settlements made use of a variety of bronze tools, made locally (Ellison 1981, p. 430). In the Levels the Middle Bronze Age continued to see extensive activity, with many trackways being built (Coles 1982).

Towards the end of the second millenium the landscape of many parts of Britain was affected by a very widespread enclosure movement. This is best exemplified by the reaves of Dartmoor, the division of the moor into great blocks of territory, sometimes over 3,000 hectares in extent. These lands were also divided internally into a coherent system of fields. In Somerset the best-documented systems are found in the north, at Cheddar, on the hills above the gorge and at Bathampton Down, near Bath (Fowler 1978, pp. 30, 36, 40). Survival here could have occurred because of the topographical conditions. There is nothing to suggest that such field systems were in use elsewhere in the region, but the very fact of their existence suggests that they were unlikely to have been isolated. Probably much of the higher open land of the north was enclosed in this way. At the same time the Levels saw a renewal of activity. As conditions became wetter new tracks were built and forest regeneration, which had begun in the late third millenium was halted and then reversed as woodland was once more coppiced (Coles 1978, pp. 86–9).

Weapons were comparatively rare as compared with tools and occur more commonly on the larger sites, such as Norton Fitzwarren (Fig. 1.4). This was a large enclosure, with a single ditch surrounding an area of about five acres (Langmaid 1971). It was on the edge of the Deverell-Rimbury and Treviskar pottery distribution areas, and probably represents a centre of exchange, under the control of high status people. A hoard found in 1970 on the same site contained items which were of continental manufacture, as well as local (Langmaid 1971, p. 119). Other hoards have been found in the Taunton area, suggesting that manufacture was concentrated in the district. Since items made in the Taunton region are to be found in Dorset and Wiltshire during this Middle Bronze Age period from 1400 to 1000 BC, we may assume that the district became prosperous. The very early hillfort may well be a sign of this wealth and a consequence of it, as high status men sought to control the wealth producing manufacture. It is noteworthy that types of weapons were widely distributed across the south of England,

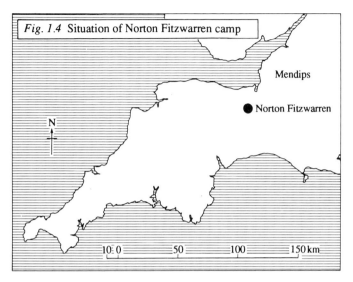

Fig. 1.4 Situation of Norton Fitzwarren camp

Mendips

● Norton Fitzwarren

N

10 0   50   100   150 km

suggesting a unity of culture and perhaps political activity at a high level in society (Ellison 1981).

The siting of the hillfort at Norton Fitzwarren may place it at the boundary between two power centres, the one based at the henge monuments upon the Mendips, the other in Devon. The hillfort might be seen as a centre of exchange, close to boundaries, where different tribal groups could meet to exchange goods, without the dangers involved in journeys deep into one another's territory.

The evidence provided by pottery finds in the early Iron Age, eighth to sixth centuries, shows that the north and east of the region were most strongly affected by the developments in Wessex (Cunliffe, 1982, p. 53). The All Canning Cross type clearly affected the pottery in use at Cadbury Castle in phases four and five and this relationship between Wessex and the material discovered in Somerset was to be maintained in succeeding centuries. Small finds from Banwell, South Stoke, Little Solsbury near Bath, Freshford and Shepton Mallet all show similar influences during the period when bronze was giving way to iron (Cunliffe 1974, p. 37). At Ham Hill the larger collection of pottery has been tentatively linked with the Kimmeridge-Caburn group, suggesting an influence from further south east (Cunliffe 1982, p. 53). In the south and west of the county very little has been found, but what there is continues the tradition of connection with the rest of the South-Western peninsula (Cunliffe 1974, pp. 35–6). The existence of the pottery suggests settlement at these sites. Those at Cadbury Castle and Ham Hill seem to have been rather large groupings, while a small enclosed settlement existed at Hayes Wood, in Freshford (Stone and Wicks 1935). The old sites in the Brue valley were also occupied at this time and Professor Coles has suggested the existence of at least five settlements in his study area (Coles 1987, p. 30). He has pointed out how much evidence has been lost in the Levels due to peat cutting. The implication is that the valley was intensively settled and that occupation was spreading, except where adverse conditions, due to increased flooding made this impossible. It seems likely that other settlement was also widespread and that the subsequent developments were built on a base of a substantial but otherwise unrecorded population.

Settlements at Chew Park Farm, Chew Valley Lake and Pagans Hill have all produced pottery comparable with the All Cannings Cross series (Apsimon *et al.* 1958) and this has been assigned to the sixth century BC (Cunliffe 1982, p. 54). During the late fifth century the hilltop settlement at Cadbury Castle received its first defences and it was quickly followed by other hillforts and defended sites throughout the region. The first rampart at Cadbury is associated with a range of ceramics which fit the Wessex sequence and other hillforts – Burledge Camp, Little Solsbury, Bathampton Down and Brean Down have all produced pottery of the same period. The sites at Ham Hill and Maes Knoll were probably also first fortified at this time (Burrow 1982) (Fig. 1.5). During the period 700–400 BC the European-wide trade network, through which prestige objects were transferred over long distances gradually ran down (Bradley 1984). As the supply of bronze items dwindled, the status of the elite was threatened and control of land and people became as important as control of exchange (Cunliffe 1984b). The use of hillforts is a measure of the social stresses produced by the changes. Although the number of forts in Somerset is partly determined by topography it may also reflect the intensity of conflict in the area. Alcock has argued that this was the result of activity by a new warrior aristocracy, continental invaders of the seventh to sixth centuries BC who brought with them new

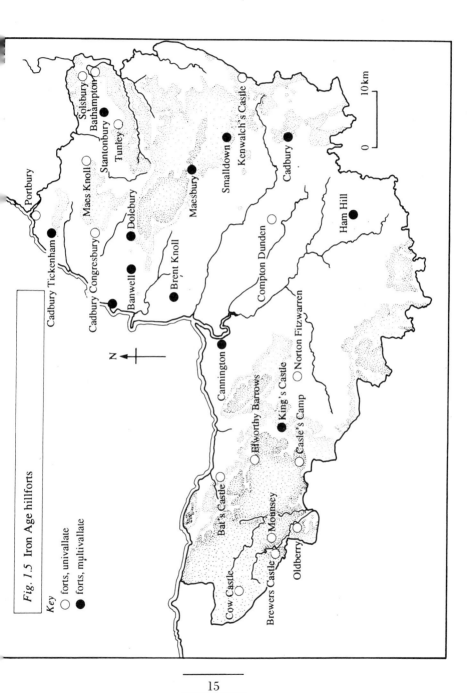

Fig. 1.5 Iron Age hillforts

Key
○ forts, univallate
● forts, multivallate

Portbury

Cadbury Tickenham

Solsbury
Bathampton
Stantonbury
Tunley
Maes Knoll
Cadbury Congresbury
Dolebury
Banwell
Brent Knoll

Kenwalch's Castle
Smalldown
Macsbury
Cadbury
Compton Dunden
Ham Hill

N

Cannington

Elworthy Barrows
King's Castle
Casle's Camp
Norton Fitzwarren

Bat's Castle
Cow Castle
Brewers Castle
Mounsey
Oldberry

10km

0

15

styles in pottery and metalwork and imposed a more rigid stratification upon society (Alcock 1987, pp. 30–2).

From the fourth century BC onward, these early forts with simple lines of defence were replaced by hillforts with extended and elaborated defences, several lines of ramparts and complex entrances. Some of the original sites were abandoned by this date, some were upgraded and others were built from new.

Over a long period refinement and development took place as the result of social and probably political changes. Initially there was a phase where many simple hillforts were constructed, wherever a suitable site was available. This was followed by a reduction in numbers and the redevelopment of the surviving, and in some cases new sites at a much more sophisticated level. All these sites show signs of intensive occupation. Regular settlements of some considerable size had developed in them and continued over a period of several hundred years before most were abandoned as fortified sites and often as dwelling sites also (Cunliffe 1982, p. 59).

Pottery described by ApSimon from Camerton, Kings Weston Down, Burledge Camp, Chew Park Farm and Pickwick Farm is similar to the pottery type associated with Alcock's rampart B, dated to the fourth to third centuries BC. Cadbury was one of the forts which were redeveloped at this time, while others went out of use. Cadbury-Congresbury, Brean Down, Burledge Camp, Little Solsbury, and Bathampton Down had been abandoned by this time, but Stokeleigh Camp, Cannington, Cadbury Castle, Ham Hill and Worlebury were redeveloped in the third-first century as were Maesbury, Blackers Hill and several others (see Fig. 1.5).

Such burdensome and intense activity as building hillforts could only have taken place in a society which was strongly structured, probably hierarchically. The building of such structures was clearly a political act, since much surplus labour was diverted into this activity: a redistributive exercise which was to the advantage of an elite. It is difficult to see any reason for such developments if they did not take place inside a society where the elite were warriors who had organised to provide themselves with signs of their status. The abandonment of some sites and the redevelopment of others on a grander scale suggests that a period of anarchic warfare was followed by a period when lesser chieftains and their subordinate groupings were defeated in the course of continuous local rivalry and absorbed into larger units, which were then able to support larger defensive sites. Evidence of the warfare comes from Worlebury, where a cemetery of mutilated bodies suggests the aftermath of a siege (Dymond 1902). Eventually such a system would develop a degree of stability, as the stronger defeated the weaker and came to agreements with those of equal strength, which would leave the large hillfort sites as political, economic and cultural centres, with their defensive role only occasionally expressed at times of political instability.

Such large works clearly needed a large infrastructure to support them. Many settlements must have existed which could have supplied chieftains with the tribute necessary to their status. The two Iron Age settlements in the Levels, the Glastonbury Lake village and the Meare villages show how large and important some settlements could be (Bulleid and Gray 1911; 1917). The Glastonbury site, which perhaps began in the fourth century BC, lay about a kilometre to the north of Glastonbury island, in the marshes, beside the river Brue, defended by a palisade (Fig. 1.6). Perhaps 100 people lived here, growing crops on the drier ground of Glastonbury island, but also keeping sheep on a large scale and manufacturing textiles. Some doubt has been expressed about whether or not this site was permanently occupied and it has been suggested that there were no huts here, only temporary structures (Barrett 1987). At the marshland site at Meare there were two settlements, West and East settlements. While settlement at the West site was in a hutted village, very like the Glastonbury Lake village, the East site was more seasonal in occupation, at least towards the end of its life. The nearby island of Meare provided fields, woodland and pastures for the communities, but the settlements were not purely agricultural and were a focus for manufacture. In particular the many glass beads, which display uniformity of pattern and chemical composition, found at the West village, suggest a substantial manufacture on the site. The finds here are the largest concentration of Iron Age glass beads found in Britain, in a non-funerary context (Coles 1987 and Henderson 1987). The manufacture of metalwork, bone utensils and textiles at the villages is also well attested. The West village site seems to have

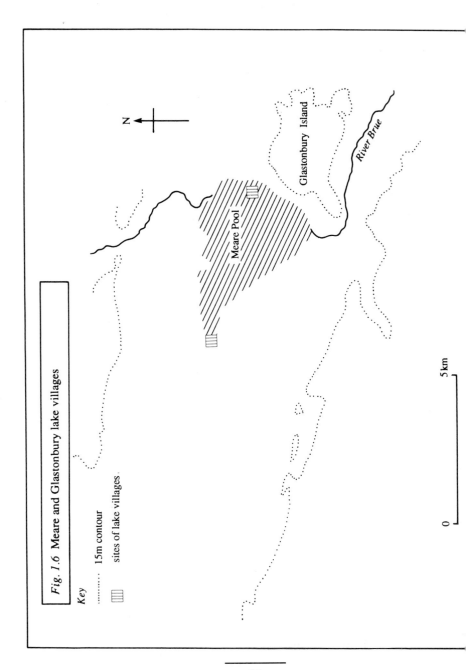

Fig. 1.6 Meare and Glastonbury lake villages

Key

.... 15m contour

⊞ sites of lake villages

0   5 km

been occupied from the third century BC and the East village from perhaps a century later and were only abandoned in the first or second centuries AD as water levels rose and the lake at Meare expanded (Coles 1987, p. 247).

From this same central district of Somerset came the 'Glastonbury ware' type of pottery which first appeared in the fourth to third centuries BC and became widespread in the whole of the South-Western peninsula, from the River Avon in the north, to Cornwall. At least six centres of production have been recognised and three of these are from Somerset (Peacock 1969). Two types of pottery, one made of sandstone material, the other of calcite, seem to have originated in central Somerset, the first near Shepton Mallet and the second close to the Mendips on the west, while a third type based upon Jurassic limestone is found scattered in the east of the county and in west Dorset and was probably made in the east of the county. The spread of this pottery, as far as Hengistbury Head for the sandstone type and into South Wales for the calcite material suggests trading links or gift exchange in both directions, while similar pottery with a fabric· originating in the Lizard region of Cornwall has been discovered in central Somerset, pointing to trading contacts with the rest of the South-Western peninsula (Peacock 1969).

The west of the county lacks similar large hillforts of the late redeveloped type, but the distribution of earlier, first phase hillfort enclosures, suggests that the west of the county passed through a similar phase of local rivalry (Burrow 1981, p. 22). Later development failed to produce large multivallate sites like Ham Hill or Maesbury, but it does not follow that it lacked a social structure of a similar type, although a different economy existed. The area is marked by the presence of many smaller enclosures, often on hill-slopes (Burrow 1981, p. 24). The pattern of west Somerset is clearly an extension of the pattern of Devon. Only Hembury stands out as an example of a later Iron Age hillfort centre of the Cadbury type (Liddel 1935; Todd 1984). The rest of the area is characterised by hill-slope enclosures, similar to those in west Somerset. These almost certainly represent settlements, perhaps associated with a pastoral economy, and may point to a major difference between the South-West, west Somerset included, and the more intensively exploited East.

The growth of industrial production in the central Somerset

area and the appearance of a local style in pottery all point to the emergence of some kind of regional culture, perhaps subsidiary to the more centralised and developed cultures of Wessex to the east. The 'Glastonbury Wares' distributed across central Somerset have already been mentioned (Peacock 1969). On Cadbury Hill the production and use of a range of luxury and high status objects such as bronze fittings from shields and iron 'currency bars', together with evidence of bronze working on the site, point to a concentration of power and wealth in the area, which suggest that if this was not the dominant central place for the centre of Somerset, then much awaits discovery elsewhere.

Religious activity in the Iron Age society of this region has left relatively few traces. The beliefs and rituals of the mass of the population are almost completely unknowable. So few burials survive from the Iron Age that it has been suggested that most corpses were disposed of by excarnation and that the few bodies discovered whole represent the disposal of people who were sacrificed or subject to special rites because they were dangerous or outcasts, people who had met violent ends, witches, suicides and the like (Wait 1985).

Two temple sites are known. At Bath it has been inferred that the cult of Sulis predates the foundation of the Roman cult and spa site in the later first century AD (Cunliffe 1985). It was part of that ubiquitous cult of healing springs, inhabited by a tutelary goddess, found throughout the Celtic world and common to the Roman world as well. At Cadbury Castle Alcock found evidence of four temple or shrine structures, two of which were probably mid to late Iron Age, the third of the second to first century BC and the last from the very end of the Iron Age, in use when the last inhabitants of the site were massacred and ejected by the Romans (Alcock 1972, pp. 163–4). It is notable that there was a temple of some sort at Cadbury Castle over many centuries and that the site falls within a group of similar temples in hillforts, oppida and population centres (Wait 1985, p. 173). Clearly the emphasis on Cadbury Castle springs from the reality of its importance in the region in the late Iron Age and beyond, not simply from the coincidence of local legend and a successful excavation. If anywhere can be seen as a 'central place' in late Iron Age Somerset, it seems to have been Cadbury Castle.

The coming of the Romans

In 121 BC the Allobroges of the Rhône valley were defeated by a Roman army near the confluence of the Rhône and the Isère. As a result the region passed under Roman control and the new Province of the Narbonensis was probably set up quite shortly thereafter (Rivet 1988, pp. 41–8). Greek traders from the *polis* of Massalia, an ally of the Romans, had already penetrated up the Rhône Valley, and it was probably through their mediation that goods from the Roman world began to spread through northern Gaul. Contacts between northern Gaul and south-eastern Britain were commonplace in the second century BC as the production of potin coins demonstrates (Haselgrove 1987). In the first century BC Roman trade spread into central and northern Gaul and from there to southern central Britain, through Hengistbury Head, which was probably a neutral trading point, with its site chosen for that reason (Hodder 1979, p. 192). This trade spread into Somerset and Mendip lead was exported via Hengistbury Head. Clearly something other than copies of Hengistbury pottery imports was received.

By the middle of the first century BC Cadbury Castle had ceased to have its defences regularly maintained, although it was not long since the last row of defences was added, and it may have ceased to be a town also (Alcock 1987, p. 176). This suggests a period of stability and expansion, in which it was possible for the rulers of local society to abandon the forts as a sign of their prestige and an insurance against the political weather.

The growth of coinage makes it possible to guess at the outline of local political authority. The coinage of the region was in circulation in the first century BC and ultimately was related to the development of long-range trade and exchange. Such a coinage is not to be regarded as 'money' in the modern sense, but rather a sign of a society where high-status individuals were involved in frequent exchange of high-value goods so that an agreed exchange rate could be maintained, and for the purposes of payment of tribute. Coins can therefore be regarded as highly specific to a group: a sign of political and social groupings (Hodder 1979, p. 191, note 56). It was not until after the invasion by Caesar in 55 BC that a tribal coinage developed in the West of Britain, since the Gallo-Belgic coins of the South-East

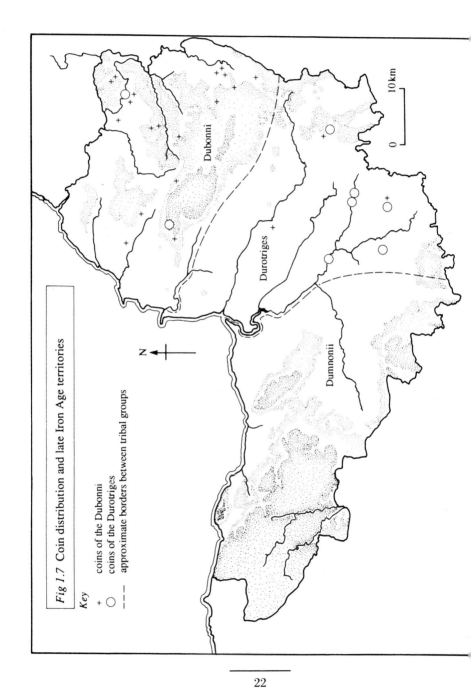

Fig 1.7 Coin distribution and late Iron Age territories

Key

+   coins of the Dubonni
○   coins of the Durotriges
– – –   approximate borders between tribal groups

Dubonni

Durotriges

Dumnonii

N

10 km

0

of Britain did not circulate widely in the West in the first half of the first century BC (Cunliffe 1974, p. 61). As coins appear it is obvious that the region was divided between the influences of tribal groupings whose centres of power lay outside the region. Dubonnic coins predominate in the north, on the Mendips and northwards, while Durotrigan coins are found in central Somerset only (Fig. 1.7). The western part of the county probably lay under the control of the Dumnonii (Cunliffe 1982). Further to the east the strains of contact with the much richer culture of the Roman world, together with the political pressures imposed by the progress of this aggressive neighbour probably explain the growth of larger territorial units, with their *oppida*. In Somerset there is no evidence that the large political groupings of the East made a deep impact. It was not until close to the time of the final Roman invasion of 43 AD that Cadbury Castle was refortified. It is unlikely that an immediate threat of invasion produced the reoccupation, since the refurbishment of the site does not seem to have been hasty. On the contrary, the place was both a fortified site and a market town, and flourished as such for perhaps fifty years (Alcock 1972, pp. 159–63). It is probable that increasing political tension caused by the growing threat from Rome, which led to political instabilities, as unsuccessful princes fled to Roman Gaul caused powerful political groupings to grow in the South-East, which in their turn had an impact on the Durotriges, expressed as a return to traditional patterns of life.

To the north, the Dubonnic part of Somerset, the Mendips northwards to the Avon valley may have been hostile to the Romans as the Durotriges were. They were split between two rulers at the time of the conquest and it appears that the northern Dubunii, in modern Gloucestershire and North Avon, were more favourably disposed to the Romans than their southern branch spread across northern Somerset and north-eastern Wiltshire (Cunliffe 1974).

When the invasion occurred Vespasian, commander of the western wing of the Roman thrust, captured about twenty *oppida*, or hillforts. Although sites such as Hod Hill and Maiden Castle in Dorset were stormed during this initial thrust, Cadbury Castle was unmolested and continued to function as a town until it was stormed and sacked in the 70s of the first century AD. It must, therefore, have submitted to Vespasian in 43–4 AD. The Roman fort at Ham Hill and the fort at Ilchester built before 49 AD point to the importance of this area in the south-east for control of the region thereafter. The Fosse Way, a military road, was constructed through Somerset by 49 AD and with it were associated forts along the road at Bath, Camerton and Shepton Mallet, with two outliers, one at Charterhouse, the centre of the lead mining operation, another at Wiveliscombe, in west Somerset and also one on Ham Hill, overlooking the Fosse Way (Leech and Leach 1982, p. 63). The whole region was now under effective Roman control, though the fortress at Ilchester was constructed after 90 AD and continued to have some role until *c*. 150 AD.

2

The Romans in Somerset

The Roman conquest

The conquest of the West of England by the legion, commanded
by the future Emperor Vespasian is not understood in detail but
it seems unlikely that the campaign could have been carried
through in a very short period. We know from written sources
that Vespasian found the campaign in Dorset hard going and
there is considerable archaeological evidence from hillforts to
substantiate this. Writing in 1976, W. H. Manning suggested
that by 47 AD the newly constructed Fosse Way represented a
militarised boundary, which divided the lowland part of Britain
from the more difficult west (1976, p. 19). More recently it has
been suggested that Roman conquest of the area, especially
where it concerned the Durotriges and the Dumnonii, was a
slow process because of the decentralised nature of their societies
(Millett 1990, pp. 51–2). Groups would have had to be conquered piecemeal and as a result it was necessary to set up forts
across the area to supervise gains. Pacification took some time
across the region and the main purpose of the road was originally
to provide a strategic rear route for the movement of troops and
supplies behind the area of active campaigning (Jones and
Mattingly 1990, pp. 93–4). The Fosse Way in Somerset is probably best understood as a communications link between a loose
spread of forts. The fort at Ilchester predates the construction of

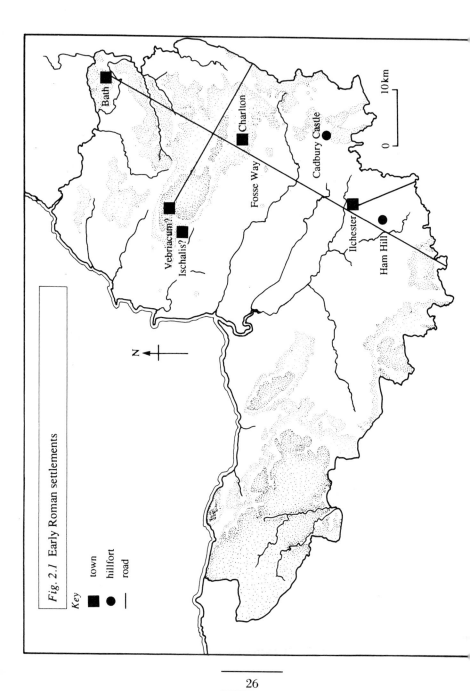

Fig. 2.1 Early Roman settlements

Key
town ■
hillfort ●
road —

Bath
Charlton
Cadbury Castle
Fosse Way
Vebriacum?
Ischalis?
Ilchester
Ham Hill
N
10 km
0

the road and so supports the idea that the road was built after the forts (Leech 1977, p. 7) (Fig. 2.1).

The hillfort of South Cadbury was the strategic key to the central area of Somerset. Once it had fallen, the land under its control, perhaps stretching to the Bristol Channel, would have fallen also. It was also a strategic site of the greatest importance for all communications to the south and to the east. The fort at Ilchester was designed to counter the power of the hillfort which continued to function as a town or perhaps an aristocratic centre for a further twenty years.

At this early stage and perhaps for long afterwards, the region remained divided between the three tribal groupings of the Dumnonii, the Durotriges and the Dubonni. To control them there was probably a fort at Ham Hill and another may have existed near Shepton Mallet, at or near the site of the recently discovered small town (Leech 1982) (see Fig. 2.1). The grouping of forts in the territory of the Durotriges is consistent with what is known of their resistance to the Romans (Millett 1990, map p. 47), while the lack of early sites among the Dubonni to the north of the Mendips may reflect their more compliant attitude towards the invaders. To the south Vespasian also undertook a campaign against the Dumnonii, something he had apparently completed by 47 AD (Salway 1981, p. 93). The fort at Exeter and its outliers, which probably included a station at Wiveliscombe were not built until *c*. 55 AD (Millett 1990, p. 50). Their existence suggests that the tribe presented a continuing problem to the Romans and was regarded as potentially troublesome.

Throughout the very early phase of Roman rule the settlement at South Cadbury continued to function. It may be that the Durotriges were initially treated as a client state, but at sometime soon after 70 AD the south-western gate at South Cadbury was stormed by Roman troops and the settlement defences destroyed. Some of the inhabitants were killed and their bodies left lying in the ditch, possibly close to where they fell (Alcock 1972, pp. 105–6). South Cadbury had become a centre for resistance to Roman authority in some localised disturbance in the 70s of the first century AD rather than at the time of the revolt of Boudicca. A small Roman garrison was installed to make sure that the site could be controlled (Alcock 1972, pp. 193–4).

It is impossible to know how quickly Roman exploitation of

Somerset proceeded, but the existence of lead pigs from the Mendips dated as early as 49 AD is a clear indication that the Roman administration intended to recoup some of the costs of the conquest as quickly as possible. These early pigs were all marked as the products of imperial mines and it was not until the reign of Vespasian (69–79 AD) that the mark of a private company appears, suggesting leasing of the site (Elkington 1976). The speed with which the lead was exploited shows that the Romans knew in advance of the existence of the deposits. As in other parts of the Empire, such as Spain and the Narbonensis it is likely that the capture of mineral resources was a prime objective of the Roman campaign. Mendip lead contains a small proportion of silver, *c.* 0·4 per cent, which was extracted on site. Exported from the Mendips, the lead was in use at distant Pompeii before 79 AD, when Vesuvius erupted. It reached Italy by sea as return cargo, by which time its price must have increased many times. The competitive edge, as compared with the lead from Spain, was that Mendip lead could be won by opencast mining, whereas the Spanish needed deep mines (Elkington 1976, p. 187). It seems likely that the labour force was initially composed of prisoners of war from the conquests in the South-West, used as slave labour, the normal practice in the Roman world. The speed with which the lead reached Italy shows how valuable it was in the ancient world but, more importantly, demonstrates the centralisation of the Empire which exploited all its resources for the benefit of Rome.

Lead working probably caused the stationing of a permanent garrison on the Mendips and a site at Charterhouse has long been known. It contained not only a small town or settlement, but also a fort and an amphitheatre (Green 1975). The name of this settlement has been identified as *Iscalis* (Rivet and Smith 1979, p. 379), but Rivet and Smith's explanation of the name in terms of the river Axe is difficult, since the river itself is several miles away and separated by a vertical distance of several hundreds of metres. It would be more sensible to see the Ptolemaic *Ischalis* as a site actually on the River Axe, perhaps at Cheddar, while the Charterhouse settlement perhaps carried the name evidenced on lead pigs, 'VEB' (Elkington 1976, p. 194), an abbreviation of a name which has been reconstructed as *Vebriacum* (Rivet and Smith 1979) (see Fig. 2.1).

28

Elsewhere the tide of early Roman occupation must have been driven by the need to control the coast, and in particular river mouths and the distant western coast. The surviving fortlets along the north Devon shore are probably related to the campaign against the Silures of South Wales (Millett 1990, p. 63). The early conquest must have used the tracks already in existence, but the construction of roads was a priority (see Fig. 2.2). The Fosse Way was constructed very early but other routes have been suggested as Roman on the basis of their relationship to Ilchester. The major routes were those along the Polden Hills to the mouth of the River Parrett and the road along the Mendips from Charterhouse to Old Sarum (Margery 1967). To the south the major communications were to the new legionary base at Exeter and to the capital of the Durotriges at Dorchester.

To the north the spring at Bath attracted Roman attention almost immediately. Pre-Flavian samian ware at Bathwick has been adduced as evidence of a possible early fort (Green 1975, p. 133), while it seems that the Fosse Way ran close to the springs (Cunliffe 1986, p. 16). A military cemetery existed on the northern side of the town and the memorial to *l. Vitellius Tancinus* of the *ala Vettonum* which was serving in South Wales suggests that the site had become a spa by the reign of Vespasian (Webster 1980, p. 87).

Small settlements developed along the roads quite quickly. To the south of Ilchester there was a small town at Westland, Yeovil, on the road to Dorchester (Leech 1977). There ought to be a further settlement along the Fosse Way south-west of Ilchester, perhaps near Chard, but there is no evidence for it as yet. However, to the north a town certainly existed in the first century at Charlton near Shepton Mallet, alongside the Fosse Way (BAFU 1990). First century coins from the area, indicating a military presence (Haverfield 1906), suggest that a detachment was first posted here, perhaps because the road from Charterhouse crossed the Fosse Way close by. This detachment was followed by a small town. Recent evidence from excavation shows that this town grew and flourished particularly in the fourth century (BAFU 1990). Further north a town grew at Camerton, possibly again built around a small fort (Wedlake 1958). The small port of Combwich at the mouth of the Parrett and the settlement at Crandon Bridge may also be early settlements.

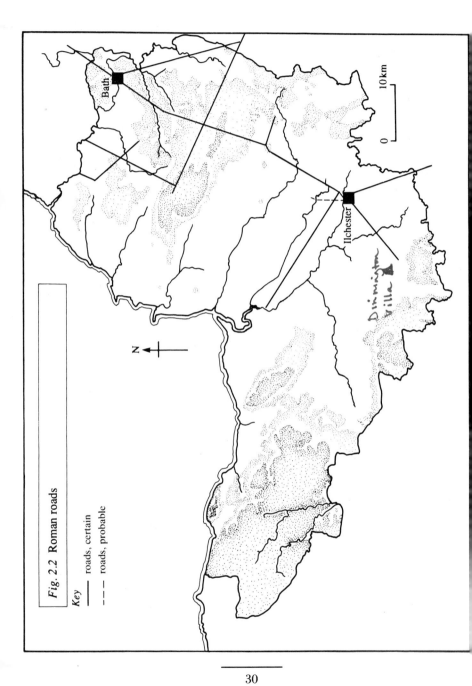

Fig. 2.2 **Roman roads**

Key
— roads, certain
- - - roads, probable

10 km

Bath

Ilchester

Dinnington Villa

N

The question of how the early administration of the region was organised after the initial Roman conquest is extremely difficult to answer. The view expressed by Professor Sheppard Frere, that urbanisation was introduced as an essential step towards local government, followed by the gradual fostering of self-government as the military moved out of an area (1987, p. 192) has recently been challenged by Martin Millet who has argued that whole tribes were turned into *civitates* piecemeal (Millett 1990, pp. 66–7). Certainly the structure of Iron Age society was such that it fitted neatly into Roman patterns, with the tribal aristocracy taking their places as the *decuriones* of the new civitates. Thus they maintained their traditional positions of power in their local society while being granted access to the wider world of Roman political and social life. It is likely that the pattern which pertained elsewhere in the Celtic world was relevant here also. Those who had taken the most prominent part against the Romans were either defeated and killed in battle or found themselves out of political favour. The factions which were inherent in such tribal aristocracies could be relied upon to throw up a party favourable to the conquerors, while the defeated group could be executed when they caused political trouble and initiated revolts, as they surely would. The problem for Somerset is that the pattern of conquest suggests that authority was weak or at least decentralised at the time of the conquest. The Romans may have altered local society by fostering the emergence of a more hierarchical structure among local aristocracy.

Town and country

Initially it seems likely that the central part of the territory, that area which belonged to the Durotriges, was administered from Dorchester. Two fourth-century inscriptions from Hadrian's Wall, one from Cawfields and the other from Housesteads refer to Ilchester; one as C(IVITAS) DUR(O)TR(I)G(UM) [L]ENDIN(I)ESIS and the other as CI(VITAS) DUROTRA(UM) LENDINIESI(S) (Rivet and Smith 1979, p. 392). On the strength of this it has been argued that the territory of the Durotriges was divided and that Ilchester became the capital of the northern part of the *civitas* (Stevens 1941). John Wacher has pointed to the creation of such *civitates* from *pagi* at Carlisle and Water Newton, as well as at Ilchester (Wacher 1974, pp. 407–8). The late date of the inscriptions fakes it very difficult to draw conclusions about the date at which this division might have taken place. A rather late date, perhaps in the late third or early fourth century might fit in with the extensive growth of population in the area.

Northern Somerset, the area which had been Dubonnic territory, seems to have been part of the civitas of the Belgae with their capital at Venta Belgarum (Winchester). It has been suggested that Bath, as the only settlement of any size in the region, may have had some larger administrative function at the western end of the very elongated territory (Green 1975, p. 137). If this is true it can only have been for the *pagus*, although clearly the exceptional site at Bath made it an outstandingly important centre of communications as well as the spa and religious centre we know it to have been.

Although the spa at Bath was provided with the temple building appropriate to its role there is little evidence that the other towns of the region were provided with lavish public buildings. The lack of dedicatory inscriptions in Bath and at Ilchester suggests that grand public buildings were not erected for competitive reasons as they were in many other parts of the Roman Empire in the early Imperial period. This would indicate that the local aristocracy formed a fairly closed oligarchy in which competition had been effectively limited (Millett 1990, p. 110). If this is indeed the case, then the towns may well have been rather utilitarian places. Capital which would otherwise have been lavished on them may have gone into the rural estates of the elite instead.

At the top of the social hierarchy are the large villas which began to appear in the mid-second century. The area around Ilchester is remarkable for the number of villas which survive. Those which were certainly of the second century and earlier are comparatively few (Leech 1977, pp. 91–105) (Fig. 2.3). The known sites are almost certainly a representative sample of all the villas of this early period in the district and their distribution and size fit well with the view that the countryside was dominated by an oligarchy. Any oligarchy, although it seeks to limit and regulate competition for control of the resources of a society,

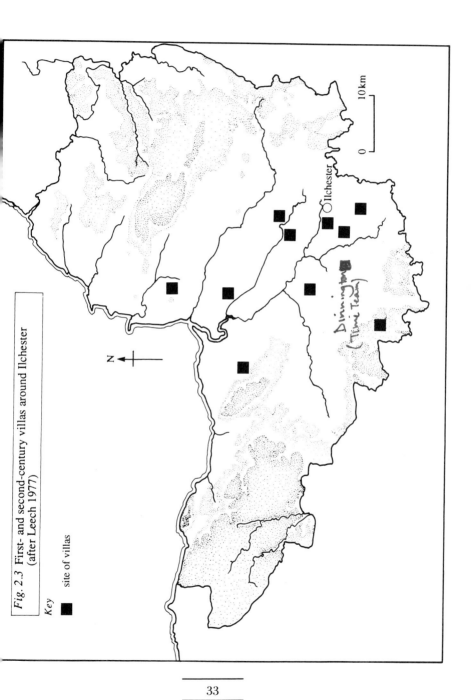

Fig. 2.3 First- and second-century villas around Ilchester
(after Leech 1977)

Key

■ site of villas

Dinnington
("Time Team")

Ilchester

N

10km

0

nevertheless is a social system within which politics are a fierce and never-ceasing activity. Only constant communication makes possible the regulation which maintains the equilibrium of the system. Since great tensions were bound to arise, a focus would be needed which was close at hand, which Ilchester provided. The need for easy communication explains why the villas further north beyond the Mendips do not look to Ilchester, but to Bath.

The aristocracy of the early Roman countryside was supported by a farming system of individual farmsteads and small hamlets which continued the pattern of Iron Age farmsteads; there was no major change in the agricultural system as a result of the Roman conquest. These farmers clearly paid rents of some type and it is unlikely that they were only subsistence farmers at the time of the Roman conquest, since coinage circulated and market centres existed. There is little evidence of the abandonment of Late Iron Age farmsteads and by the second century new farming settlements began to appear, indicating that capital was being invested in the countryside (Leech 1982). From most early farm sites in Somerset samian ware is a diagnostic feature. The importation of this fine ware on such a large scale indicates that money flowed into the hands of farmers, as well as into the pockets of the aristocracy. By the second century the elite group were almost certainly financing the creation of new agricultural settlements, such as that at Catsgore, near Ilchester, which was founded c. AD 100–120. Some twenty settlements of this type have been recognised in central Somerset and this suggests that the second century was a time of expansion in agriculture and probably also of population (Leech 1982, p. 225). In addition, the drainage of marshland close to the sea around Brent Knoll, in the marshes of the Axe valley and north of the Mendips around the villa site at Wemberham suggests that money was being invested in large-scale operations. The investors would expect a return on the capital employed.

The commercialised landscape of central Somerset is probably repeated in the area north of the Mendips. The farm at Row of Ashes Farm, Butcombe continued to function as a Late Iron Age establishment which underwent rebuilding with rectangular instead of round buildings at the end of the first century AD (Fowler 1968; 1970). This site has produced some indications of Roman military equipment as well as the ubiquitous samian ware. At Chew Valley there is strong evidence of an expansion of agricultural activity, especially extension of grain cropping (Rahtz and Greenfield 1977). The picture in the northern part of the county is complicated by the possible existence of an Imperial estate at Combe Down, just outside Bath, but this may have had more to do with stone quarries than agriculture (Frere 1987, p. 267).

The region which was least affected by the rise of the villa system lay on the western side of the Parrett and the Tone. Here villa sites seem to have been non-existent. Grinsell, writing in 1970, identified only one villa west of the Parrett, at Spaxton (Grinsell 1970, p. 96) (see Fig. 2.3). Other non-villa sites clearly existed. Grinsell noted evidence for settlement at Doniford, near Watchet, but the evidence of field names suggests that settlement was much more widely spread. Field names such as 'blackland', 'chisels', 'chester', 'cinderlands' and 'crocks' are certainly not infallible guides to hitherto unknown Roman-period sites – indeed they sometimes occur on much older sites – but they do give a guide to the frequency of early settlement. At least eighteen parishes in the area have such field names, suggesting that minor farms and similar sites were not uncommon (Fig. 2.4).

The developed pattern which existed by the mid-third century was of a settled and well-developed countryside with several thriving towns. There is considerable evidence that the clayland belt in the west-central part of Somerset as well as the clayland area to the north of the Mendips was drained and protected from flooding. The region around Brent Knoll and the Axe Valley were probably turned into grazing grounds and settlements developed there (Leech 1982, p. 231–2). The number of villa sites continued to grow, although the new dwellings were not generally as large as the first wave of building, demonstrating the downward spread of wealth among the aristocracy and the probable increase in the size of that class.

The villa site at Gatcombe is a very good example of the scale and complexity of such a settlement (Fig. 2.5). Here the villa began in the late third century and continued to function for about a century, being abandoned in the 360s (Branigan 1977, p. 177). The whole site was provided with a strong defensive wall, perhaps necessary because of the proximity of the Bristol Channel and the possibility of attacks by pirates. Excavations

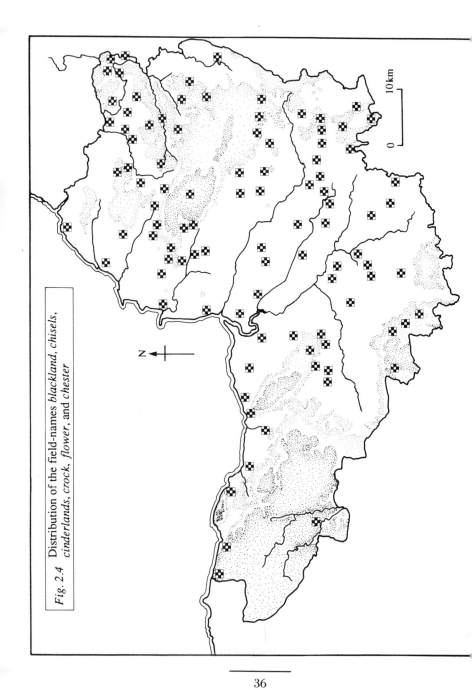

Fig. 2.4 Distribution of the field-names *blackland*, *chisels*, *cinderlands*, *crock*, *flower*, and *chester*

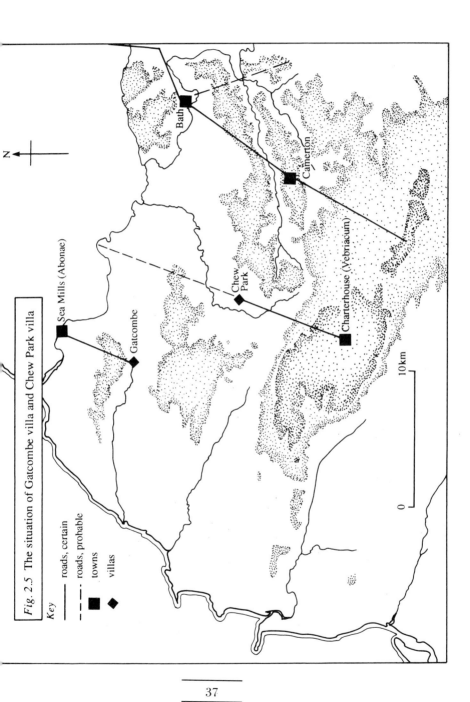

Fig. 2.5 The situation of Gatcombe villa and Chew Park villa

Key

roads, certain
roads, probable
towns
villas

Sea Mills (Abonae)

Gatcombe

Bath

Camerton

Chew Park

Charterhouse (Vebriacum)

N

0   10km

were concentrated upon the farm buildings, the villa itself having been destroyed in the nineteenth century by a railway cutting. It has been suggested that the estate attached to the villa may have been as large as 15,000 acres (Branigan 1977, p. 195). Such a settlement might have needed as many as fifty or sixty families to provide the workforce (Branigan 1977, p. 199), Other villa estates in the region were not as big as Gatcombe and would have needed fewer workers. Large villas, such as Low Ham or Wemberham may well have been the centres of similar grand estates which reflected the wealth and power of the very topmost layer of the tribal aristocracy.

There are, however, difficulties in the interpretation of the Gatcombe site. Other villas do not have a large wall around them. An alternative suggestion is that this site was a state-controlled depot for the reception and processing of agricultural produce and metals (Esmonde Cleary 1989, p. 48). If this were the case, then the wall would be explained and the suggestions about the large estate attached to this unit would be superfluous. However, such an explanation itself needs some justification when viewed geographically. Gatcombe is in fact rather isolated; it is not close to a major road; it does not stand in an area of outstanding productivity; it is not close to a major urban centre, where produce could be sold or shipped. On balance, interpretation as a private rather than a public site seems preferable.

In contrast with the large complex at Gatcombe, the villa at Chew Park, not far away, was first occupied in the Roman period by a wooden farmhouse. This stood on a site which had long been in use in the Iron Age, so that the timber farmhouse may represent a switch to a new style of living when the house was built. This house was superseded in its turn by a stone farmhouse built in the later third century, although the wooden house may have been abandoned before the stone house was constructed (Rahtz and Greenfield 1977, pp. 33–53) (see Fig. 2.5). Such a sequence probably demonstrates in a general way the growth of incomes from small to medium estates.

The overall picture is of a countryside in which the large romanised houses of the aristocracy were a prominent feature. We do not understand the relationship between these villas and the lands around them. It is very easy to assume that each villa was surrounded by lands which were directly owned by the proprietor of the villa. If that is the case, then much of central and northern Somerset would have been directly in the hands of large landed proprietors, drawing income from large numbers of tenant farmers. Such a pattern would fit well with the position in many other parts of the western Roman Empire. On the other hand the tenurial relationship between villa owners and the peasantry may have been more complicated, with the survival and development of personal ties of dependency or physical relationship, so that ownership of an estate was expressed more in terms of personal obligations than in ownership of the soil. The survival of a part of a document written on wood, discovered in a well at the Chew Park villa, may well be important (Rahtz and Greenfield 1977, p. 63). What survives is part of a document relating to the sale of real estate, using the normal forms of Roman civil law. It seems reasonable to assume that it refers to property in the area. This and the survival of the use of Roman forms in the sixth-century charters of Llandaff suggest that a commercial landmarket existed. What we cannot know is the place of the peasantry inside such a market. The close spacing of villas in the region certainly suggests that if each had an estate attached to it, then the boundaries of the estates met one another, and that there was little or no room for small independent peasant proprietors. Whether such a view is also tenable for the Dumnonian regions west of the Parrett-Tone line we cannot say, but a system of rural lordship or ownership by an aristocracy seems the most likely model.

Evidence for the connection between villas and other, non-villa settlements has been summarised by Richard Hingley (1989, pp. 102–10). In other parts of the western Empire, notably in Gaul, it has been demonstrated that some very large villas had lesser villas within their sphere of influence, as well as non-villa settlements. We do not yet have evidence for such a hierarchy in Somerset. The survival of a pattern of settlement which flows directly from the pattern of late villa distribution, and which in essentials preserves the social relationship between villa (or its successor) and the settlements around it has been suggested for other parts of the country and represents a major part of the argument of the following two chapters of this book.

In other parts of Britain the towns of this period exhibit considerable development. By the mid-third century the rural aristocracy had moved into the towns and built themselves substantial houses. At Ilchester the early timber-framed houses were replaced with more substantial stone buildings from the late second/early third centuries and by the fourth century there is evidence of elegant houses with mosaic floors. The later town had also developed suburbs which spread well outside its defences (Leach 1982, p. 8). These late second or early third century earth ramparts were built at a time when many other towns in Britain were also building walls. Clodius Albinus, who was proclaimed Emperor in Britain and defeated by Septimus Severus near Lyon in 196, may have ordered the construction of the walls as part of his plan to withdraw troops from Britain and set out to substantiate his claim to the purple (Wacher 1974, p. 75). Once constructed, prestige probably kept the ramparts standing until, in the fourth century, they became of more practical use. Ilchester was almost certainly a market and political centre, with minor manufacturing. Excavation has produced evidence for lead, bronze and iron working. The town acted as a distribution centre for pottery traded from abroad in the early period and then, as long distance trade in pottery declined from the late third century, New Forest and Oxfordshire wares were traded. There was a considerable pottery manufacture in the lower Axe and Brue valleys (Leach 1982, pp. 40–1) in a region which not only provided suitable raw materials, but was near the edge of *civitas* boundaries, which may have helped in the distribution. Ilchester probably provided an outlet for this material as well. Its population may have reached 2,000 to 3,000 people by the third century (Leach 1982, p. 10). A similar sized population probably existed at the town at Charlton. The recent excavations have shown that manufacturing of metal work also took place there, and it seems likely that the newly discovered settlement was much like Ilchester in its economic functions. Further north again, the town at Camerton exhibits the same developments as occurred at Ilchester. A settlement of timber-framed houses was replaced in the late second century by stone buildings. In the middle of the third century the settlement expanded as it developed manufacturing industry. Furnaces for smelting iron were built, probably to take advantage of the cheap local coal which was available and using iron ore from the Forest of Dean. The other metal industry at Camerton was the production of pewter. Plenty of lead was available from the Mendip mines and the tin may have come from Cornwall. The result was a substantial manufacturing industry (Wedlake 1958). Pewter was also made at Lansdown, near Bath, again probably using the lead from the Mendips (Frere 1987, p. 283).

At Bath the site of the sacred bath first developed in the later years of the first century, with the erection of the Temple of Sulis Minerva and the management of the spring itself. In the early second century the main temple precinct was remodelled on a larger scale, with a *tholos* and, at the beginning of the fourth century, a further redevelopment resulted in the enclosure and roofing over of the spring. This sacred complex formed the heart of Roman Bath. Together the temple complex and the associated spring must have formed a group of buildings far grander than anything else in the west of Britain and comparable with many of the more sophisticated centres to be found on the mainland of the western Empire. Professor Barry Cunliffe doubted that Bath could be seen as a town, but suggested that it was an enclosed sacred site, with a wall probably built after AD 300 (Cunliffe 1986, pp. 21–41). However, the scale of the sacred bathing establishment must have supported a substantial population, if only to supply the needs of visitors. The Roman road sytem of the region concentrates routes at Bath, which became an important road junction. In addition, there is some evidence for the clustering of villa sites around Bath, which would suggest that it acted as a social, political and economic focus throughout the whole Roman period. The use of Bath stone for the columns on the villa at Bignor shows that the stone was sufficiently well known and highly valued that long distance transport of quite large quantities could be undertaken (Frere 1987, p. 288).

The small port at Combwich was perhaps too small to be a fully-fledged town, but it probably provided an outlet for goods and a means of communication between the region and South Wales. It seems likely that it served the region to the west of the River Parrett (Rahtz 1969).

All these towns, except Combwich, are on the Fosse Way. The initial road system, provided in the course of the conquest, retained its importance. Indeed the line of the Fosse Way was to provide the axis along which the densest population and the richest territory was to lie right through the medieval period, as well as the Roman. In addition the basic road pattern was filled out, particularly in the north, where roads have been located in the area south of the Avon valley, suggesting a concentration of population (Margery 1967, p. 84). But the roads we customarily call 'Roman' are roads which are distinguished as having been laid out and constructed in a uniform manner, normally with metalling and proper foundations. Many other less well-constructed roads and tracks must have been in use, especially as the countryside filled up with farms, settlements and villas. It has been suggested that much of the present network of roads survives from the Roman period (Leech 1977, p. 184). Certainly a widespread system must have existed and some parts of it probably survived into much later times, unrecognised by us.

The gods

We have little coherent knowledge of the religious beliefs which the Romans found in the area in the middle of the first century, but it can be assumed that pantheistic cults of the type common throughout Celtic western Europe were popular here also. It seems likely that the focus of aristocratic centres was upon gods who protected established groups and who sanctioned existing political arrangements and such gods were most vulnerable when the structure of local politics went through a crisis. The Durotrigan settlement at South Cadbury certainly lost its shrine when the site was destroyed and the inhabitants displaced in the 70s AD (Alcock 1972, p. 171). However, gods with healing powers would escape a loss of prestige and the site at Bath was taken in hand by the conquerors as a holy site almost immediately. In itself it was representative of a belief in the holy quality of springs which was common to the whole of western Europe, a belief which the Romans fully shared with their new subjects. Throughout the region 'holy wells' are extremely common and some may have survived as holy sites in an unbroken line into the modern period. At South Cadbury, for instance, the holy well on the side of the hillfort was still credited with magical powers in the seventeenth century, when, in 1634, a group of local girls were accused in the consistory court of obscene behaviour, among them 'Joanna Perrie ffor that she, with diverse other women of the same parish did on a certain

Sabbath day within this moneth last and during prayer time goe upp to the castell theare in which being a well, they did baptize themselves and named nyne Counts and longe prickes and such like' (D/D/Ca. 300). This is one of many holy well sites which have survived. Some are probably medieval in origin, but others may link the medieval period with a mode of belief common to most men and women in the Roman period. By no stretch of the imagination could one see the South Cadbury well as merely a 'popish superstition' as did the contemporaries of Joanna Perrie.

At Bath the site was made especially holy by the fact that the powerful spring was also hot. It clearly had a connection with the underworld which was seen as being close and energetic. The Romans were happy to recognise the local goddess Sulis as cognate with their own Minerva and the cult received official backing and the romanisation of the spring was carried through in the decade AD 60–70. Professor Barry Cunliffe has made it clear that until that time a military road ran close to the site and has suggested that the romanisation of the site was a deliberate act of reconciliation (Cunliffe 1986, p. 21). This was the only romanised temple in the region and had an importance which spread far beyond the locality. The temple to Sulis Minerva, built next to the spring, was dedicated in Latin. It represented a Roman cult which embraced the native Celtic cult and brought it into the Roman world (Cunliffe 1985). The thermal medical establishment which grew up and remained popular at least until the second half of the fourth century was of international standing. However, that should not obscure the fact that this was a religious establishment which had its own *haruspex*. People came to worship the goddess at the pool and in the temple, and pilgrims who came to be cured came with a religious motive. The curses found in the pool, written on small lead sheets, together with the thousands of ritually offered coins show the liveliness of belief in the powers of the goddess among ordinary people. They sought help with ordinary things of everyday life: the recovery of lost or stolen property and the punishment of wrongdoers.

No other town in the region has produced evidence of a temple. The implication is that religious practice among the indigenous population remained close to home, in the country-side. The local oligarchy was able to regulate competition among themselves, so that they did not need to decorate the towns with romanised religious buildings to establish their standing in the community, while official colonists – who might be expected to acknowledge imperial power or generosity – were absent.

It is likely that small local shrines, perhaps attached to villas, were important. As the rural aristocracy became romanised they seem to have adopted the gods of the Romans. At West Coker the finds at the villa included a bronze plaque to Mars Rigisamus and a statue of the god (Leech 1977, p. 127). A temple to the god has been suggested for this site (Ross 1967, p. 175). The Keynsham villa contained evidence of Emperor worship as well as the god Silvanus (Green 1976), while the Pitney villa mosaics contained representations of Neptune, Mercury and of Mithras. This last is some evidence for a cult which, as a foreign mystery, developed a following among soldiers and had important temples in other parts of Britain; the nearest known dedication to the god being at Caerleon (Jones and Mattingley 1990, map 8:21). At Whatley, the villa mosaics included a picture of the goddess Cybele. Her cult was also an exotic import, from Anatolia (Green 1976). Such a cult might suit a cultivated member of the aristocracy, but it is difficult to imagine that it could appeal to the peasants of the countryside.

In the late third century the region was distinguished by the appearance of a series of rural temples (Fig. 2.6). The first of these was at Pagan's Hill, Chew Stoke, where an octagonal temple was accompanied by a range of buildings which may have been accommodation for the devotees, and a well which probably had a ritual purpose (Rahtz 1951, pp. 112–42; Rahtz and Harris 1958, pp. 15–32). Two other sites have been excavated, at Lamyatt Beacon, built c. AD 300 (Leech 1980) and at Brean Down, dated to c. AD 340 (ApSimon et al. 1960–61). At Lamyatt the discovery of eight statuettes of gods, including two of Mercury, one of Mars, one Minerva, one of Hercules and a *Paterfamilias* suggest that romanised cults were again popular. Both revealed conventional Roman-Celtic temples and both stood on isolated hilltops. At Henley Wood, near Yatton, a temple stood on top of another hill. This was erected in the first half of the third century and continued to stand until the end of the fourth century. Other possible temple sites have been identified at South Cadbury, where the discovery of a gilt-bronze letter 'A' and many coins of the late third and fourth centuries

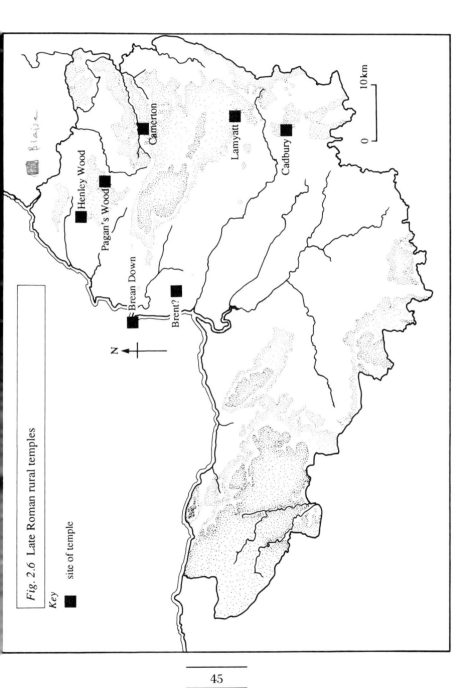

Fig. 2.6 Late Roman rural temples

Key

■ site of temple

N

Blaise

Henley Wood

Pagan's Wood

Brean Down

Brent?

Camerton

Lamyatt

Cadbury

0   10 km

suggest a late third century foundation (Alcock 1972, pp. 173–74) and at Camerton, from the first half of the third century. Evidence noted by the Rev. Skinner in the early nineteenth century suggests that a building stood on the summit of Brent Knoll. He found painted wall plaster and roof tiles. A temple seems the most likely building for a site which is too exposed and uncomfortable for a dwelling, as well as difficult of access (Burrow 1981, p. 143). There are probably other sites of the same kind awaiting discovery.

We can only speculate on the social circumstances which led to the construction of these temples. At Cadbury the site probably retained strong links with the past identity of local people, but Lamyatt, Brean and Yatton were not hillfort sites. It is possible that the dedication of the sites at Brean and at Yatton was not to a romanised god, but to a British deity. It is noteworthy that both at Brean and at Chelvey near Henley Hill, the parishes churches are dedicated to St Bridget, a very rare dedication in England. There is a possibility that this is, in fact, a reference to the goddess Brigantia, a possibility reinforced by the derivation of the name of the hillfort near to Brean, Brent Knoll. Both names have been derived from the British *briga*, which meant 'a high place' (Ekwall 1960), as well as refering to the goddess (Ross 1967, p. 360). Clearly such buildings would have been erected with the authority of men of substance and it is tempting to see them as representing 'estate temples', put up as part of the dominance pattern of important local aristocrats. As with later churches, patronage of the means of access to the spiritual world enhanced the prestige and the social authority of important men. The temples serve to emphasise the importance of the rural nobility and point to the stability of their social control over the countryside. It is noteworthy that the movement which produced these country temples spanned a period from the first half of the third century until at least the late fourth century. It was not an ephemeral phenomenon, but something deeply rooted in the mature Roman countryside.

Christianity was another eastern mystery religion, brought in by the long distance movement of peoples through the western Empire. Although its presence has been suggested in villas at Frampton, Hinton St Mary and Fifehead Neville in Dorset from the fourth century, as a result of the discovery of mosaic representations of Christ and other Christian symbols (Thomas 1981, pp. 104–6), the imagery in Somerset mosaics is less convincing. Doves occur in the villa at Keynsham and dolphins, fish, panthers and peacocks in the villa at Wellow. Although it is clear that symbols such as these often had an allegorical significance by the fourth century, we cannot be certain that they are signs of Christianity (Morris 1983, p. 15). Neither are there any signs of church buildings inside the towns. The late Roman cemeteries which have been identified within the county all raise considerable problems. Professor Philip Rahtz has explored and classified the cemeteries known for the region, including Somerset (Rahtz 1977, pp. 53–64). The implication of his work is that although west-east graves without mortuary goods became the norm in the Late Roman world of Somerset, we should be cautious about ascribing such cemeteries to Christians, at least at this early date.

However, we are not totally without evidence. Of particular importance is the discovery of a small cemetery at the Roman town near Shepton Mallet (BAFU 1990). All the burials, fifteen in number, were orientated east-west with their heads to the west. The provisional date for this cemetery is late fourth to early fifth century and it is noteworthy that it was enclosed within its own boundary ditch and lay on the edge of the settlement. Here one of the graves contained a burial with a small amulet cross associated with the body. Such a find must encourage the idea that other similar cemeteries existed at other Roman towns in Somerset at this period and that Christianity was commonplace even if not the only religious belief. Clearly this cemetery was too small to have contained the burials of more than a small community of Christians and pagan cemeteries of contemporary date have also been discovered nearby.

The association of an early Anglo-Saxon church site with an extramural cemetery at Ilchester (Dunning 1974) suggests that Christians were buried there also while the town still functioned, while the remarkable association between the much later Anglo-Saxon chapel at Wells and the earlier mausoleum structure of a late Roman date argues strongly for a continuity of knowledge of and use of such sites for Christian purposes over a long period (Rodwell 1982). It seems unlikely that men of the Anglo-Saxon period would have sought out and used these places as Christian sites if there were not some long Christian association attached to them.

At Bath an pagan altar dedicated in the fourth century by a centurion carries the inscription *locum religiosum per insolentiam erutum.virtute et n(umini) Aug(usti) repurgatum reddidit G.Seuerius Emeritus c(enturio) reg(ionarius)* 'a holy spot wrecked by insolent hands and cleansed afresh, Gaius Severius Emeritus centurion in charge of the region has restored to the Virtue and Deity of the Emperor' (Collingwood and Wright 1965, no. 152). Clearly the man who restored the monument or the temple did so in some official capacity at a time when the Empire was not officially Christian. His position may well have been akin to the chief of police. It has been suggested that the damage was the work of militant Christians (Thomas 1981, p. 136). We might expect Christianity to exist in such a sophisticated place, but equally it is likely that the old gods died very hard and that Sulis Minerva and the other gods associated with the sacred spring continued to be followed until the end of the fourth century. Even at the end of the fourth century the temple precinct was being roughly patched and it may not have been until the early fifth century that the Gorgon head from the temple facade was used in paving (Cunliffe 1986, pp. 47–8).

If there were substantial numbers of Christians to be found in towns such as Ilchester or perhaps Bath we might expect that there would have been a bishop associated with one or other of these communities, since this was the normal pattern in the late Roman world (Frend 1982). However, if such officials existed, they have left no trace behind. One might have expected that some evidence of such organisation might have survived from the fourth century into the period of written evidence beginning with the coming of Christianity to the Anglo-Saxons in 597. Of course bishops did exist inside the Celtic church, usually living in monasteries, but they have left no evidence in our region. On the continent the bishops survived because towns survived. Here they did not. It is likely that bishops went down with their towns in our region or moved away as they were deserted.

It is not possible to say that by the end of the fourth century Christianity was the only or even the dominant religion of the area. The continuance of some kind of pagan belief and practice is almost certain and paganism certainly carried over into the post-Roman period. The temple at Pagans Hill shows signs of use into the fifth century, although the temple at Brean Down was out of use by *c.* AD 370 (ApSimon *et al.* 1960–61) and Lamyatt Beacon by the end of the century. We must remember that the continuance of belief and even practice was not contingent upon the continuance of the temples. Although the temples may have fallen into disuse because of changes in belief, they may equally well have been the victim of a loss of financial support as the result of the change in circumstances of a wealthy patron. Worship could go on in private houses or at open sites and probably did.

Conclusions

Until at least the middle of the fourth century and probably beyond, there is every indication that Somerset was a quiet, well-ordered and relatively prosperous part of the Roman world. Remarkably little had happened to disturb the layout which the pattern of conquest and then of development through the road system had imposed on the region. There is no reason to think that the later county of Somerset had yet any form inside the Roman region. To the north, Bath was still inside another *civitas* as was the region to the west of the Parrett-Tone line. Ilchester, in so far as it continued to be of importance in the fourth century was still the focus of the region. Although Ilchester itself was to suffer an eclipse in the sub-Roman period this district was to retain its importance because of its position on the Fosse Way and its relationship with the land to the east. By the mid-fourth century the region had the largest population it had ever had or was to have for many centuries. This alone was a measure of its success. But the world of order and calm was to be destroyed and a new order established, within which for the first time the outline of the medieval world can be discerned.

C

3

Post-Roman Somerset:
catastrophe and collapse

Few things excite the imagination more than the prospect of finding buried treasure. The crock of gold at the end of the rainbow was a reality for some of our ancestors, and it seems that in Somerset the chance of finding a fortune was high. Elsewhere in the western empire, precious metal hoards from the late fourth to early fifth centuries are rare but they are comparatively common in Britain, especially in the South-West. Of the sixty-six separate hoards listed by Archer (1979, pp. 33–64), no less than fifteen (over 20 per cent) are in the historic county of Somerset (Fig. 3.1). With a further four in Wiltshire, one in Dorset and one in Devon, a total of 31 per cent of all finds are in the region. In addition, the existence of the Old English field-name **goldhord** in two places on the Polden Hills suggests that our ancestors got there first (Egerton 3321).[1] We have only a sample of the hoards buried and not found subsequently.

Why should so many hoards occur here and not elsewhere? We know that it was not an especially wealthy area, although it had a high concentration of villas. Gloucestershire was also rich, yet only one hoard is reported from there. Ten of the fifteen datable Somerset hoards were buried between *c*. AD 390 and *c*. AD 400 and since twenty-five of the forty-two dated hoards from all over

---

[1] The manuscript BL Egerton 3321 is an early fourteenth century survey of the lands of Glastonbury Abbey. Many early field-names are preserved in it.

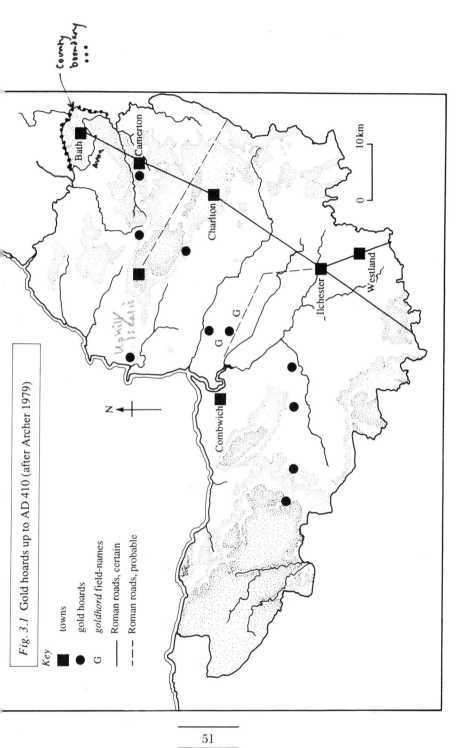

Fig. 3.1 Gold hoards up to AD 410 (after Archer 1979)

Key

■ towns

● gold hoards

G *goldhord* field-names

—— Roman roads, certain

– – – Roman roads, probable

Bath

Camerton

Charlton

Westland

Ilchester

Combwich

N

G
G

county boundary ...

uphill is calis

10km

0

51

Britain fall within these dates it is clear that the Somerset group reflects a pattern common to the whole of Britain.

Gold and silver was minted and issued by the Roman state to pay its soldiers and officials; it was also what the state demanded for its taxes. The precious metal currency was to a large extent the coin of government and officialdom. People outside government circles coveted it and used it as a standard of reference but the coin was not issued for their benefit. Failure of the coinage was, therefore, a symptom of the failure of the Roman state. Few hoards were deposited after c. AD 410 because no more coin came into the country. After this date soldiers and officials were no longer being paid in Britain and taxes were no longer being collected in coin (Esmonde Cleary 1989, pp. 140–1). Furthermore, the issues of bronze coin, used by most people for everyday transactions, also ceased. On earlier occasions when this had happened counterfeit coins were put into circulation, meeting a need for a medium of exchange (Esmonde Cleary 1989, pp. 95–6). After AD 400 this substitute was not produced. With the departure of Roman administration and troops two or three years after the passage of the usurper Constantine III to the continent in AD 407 Britain ceased to be an effective part of the Roman Empire in the west. The evidence suggests that the money economy collapsed precipitously. Once precious metal ceased to be imported its real value soared. People stopped spending their money and hoarded it instead, since it had become too valuable to use. If money ceased to circulate almost overnight, this may have been the last gasp of an economy which had been ailing for some time. Ordered Roman life had been breaking up for at least twenty years before the final act.

Writing in 1976, Branigan suggested that some of the Somerset villas were destroyed by fire in AD 367 as a result of the 'Barbarian Conspiracy' (Branigan and Fowler 1976, pp. 94–5). More recently that interpretation for the villas in central and south Somerset has been attacked by Dr R. H. Leech (1977, pp. 202–3). At Ilchester Mead, Lufton and Catsgore there is evidence of hearths or ovens built on the mosaic floors, while at Bradley Hill occupation continued into the early fifth century. At Chew Park, on the other hand, the excavator considered that the farm had ceased to be used not long after the middle of the fourth century (Rahtz and Greenfield 1977, p. 64), while at

Gatcombe the site has been interpreted as having been abandoned abruptly *c*. 370 AD and then reoccupied a few years later, with coin evidence continuing up to *c*. 402 AD. The later occupation was on a smaller scale than that of the first phase and probably continued well into the fifth century (Branigan 1977, p. 178).

There is no doubt that the villa at Keynsham suffered a catastrophic fire in the fourth century, during which a wall collapsed. It is not clear whether the skeleton found under the wall was of a body already lying there or was of someone caught and killed in the collapse (Bulleid and Horne 1926). This site was reoccupied some time later, long enough after the fire for the rubble of the wall and the body to remain undisturbed. At Brislington, a little further west, the skeletons of four or five people were recovered from a well, where they had evidently been tipped as rubbish. Here the site was abandoned before 370 AD and then reoccupied at a later date (Branigan 1972). Near Bath, both the Combe Down and Wellow II villas were said to show traces of fire damage (Haverfield 1906, pp. 314–15). This may of course be true, although the excavation of these buildings took place at the beginning of the nineteenth century and techniques of examination and interpretation have improved since that date. The much larger villa at Wellow (Wellow I), a most impressive building of 248 ft by 262 ft, did not suffer fire damage and was reported as producing coins of Valentinian (364–75). It is unlikely that the smaller house would have been attacked and destroyed and not the larger one. It seems more likely either that buildings burnt down when they were no longer properly looked after, or that fire damage which occurred late in the history of the buildings was never rectified.

It seems reasonable to suggest that while some villas in the Avon valley may have suffered damage in the mid-fourth century, most continued to function until near the end of the century. In some cases buildings may have stood empty for a time or fallen into decay, but many were reoccupied on a reduced scale. The sharp decline of the money economy drastically reduced the incomes of villa owners, who could no longer pay for specialist maintenance on their villas. Eventually, the owners were reduced to camping in their houses and thereafter abandoned them in favour of dwellings which were more appropriate to the reduced technology of the time.

Rural settlements, such as Catsgore, were probably more resilient than villas but they also became deserted, although here the desertion took place much later, perhaps in the early fifth century (Leech 1977, pp. 77–8). Other putative larger agricultural settlements have not been excavated, but if, for example, the site at Charlton Mackrell reported by Haverfield (1906, p. 323) is a village, and not a villa, the discovery of forty coins with a terminus in the reign of Theodosius (379–95), points to occupation of such a site until the very late fourth century. Dr R. H. Leech has suggested that something like half of all Romano-British rural settlements around Ilchester were finally abandoned. It is very difficult to define with any precision exactly when this took place, but it seems to be during the fifth century (1977, pp. 204–6). He has argued for continuity of occupation in some cases, so that later hamlets and villages may cover Romano-British sites, but the desertion of so many other places suggests that there was a fall in the population.

The towns present a very similar picture. At Ilchester coins continue until the reigns of Honorius and Arcadius (395–408). The excavator has tentatively suggested that some material from the town can be dated 'beyond the early 5th century' and that the settlement flourished into the early decades of the fifth century (Leach 1982, p. 12). There is some very slight evidence which may tie the site into the renewed activity at Cadbury Castle, but this does not prove the continuance of any kind of town life.

At Bath, the temple precinct was kept in good repair until after the mid-fourth century when the standard of maintenance began to decline (Cunliffe 1985, p. 184). Repair continued into the early fifth century, using slabs from the temple pediment, including the Gorgon's head. In other parts of the town occupation continued well into the fifth century and perhaps even into the sixth (Cunliffe 1986, pp. 47–9).

Although Ilchester and Bath continued to be inhabited, we do not know to what extent they retained urban characteristics. Both may have been no more than large farming settlements. On the other hand either may have retained some residual function as a meeting place or religious centre. This last seems highly probable. At Bath the later monastic foundation of early or mid-eighth century date was sited in the temple-bath complex, suggesting that traces of its function as a ceremonial centre were still evident. The Anglo-Saxon Chronicle for 577 records the capture of the 'city' of Bath. At Ilchester the later minster church at Northover stood beside a cemetery of the fourth century (Dunning 1974, p. 228), suggesting that continuity of some kind, perhaps for religious purposes, had occurred.

The smaller towns seem to have declined in parallel with the bigger settlements. Provisional views about the town at Shepton Mallet suggest a prosperous late fourth century, followed by a period when some wooden buildings succeeded the stone built houses (BAFU 1990). At Camerton, Wedlake suggested that the settlement continued to be occupied to the end of the fourth century, with 'squatters' in the fifth century. Material from the cemetery confirms this continued occupation (Wedlake 1958, p. 97).

The major difficulty faced by all archaeologists for the fifth century is the paucity of material. Traces of occupation and artifacts are extremely difficult to find and the general conclusion must be that the production of manufactured goods of all types declined sharply. This is particularly the case for pottery. No manufacturing sites are known for the fifth century and there is no evidence that new pottery was available (Esmonde Cleary 1989, p. 154). People must have used up old supplies and then turned to wooden and leather utensils.

The inference to be drawn from all this evidence is that the early fifth century saw a complete dislocation of the economy at all levels of society. No one was unaffected. Aristocrats in villas and their tenants and servants on their estates, merchants in the towns and the artisans who made goods for sale were all hit by the disappearance of the settled economy of the fourth century and the withdrawal of Roman administration. In this situation the burial of treasure was a rational response to what happened. It is likely that social unrest and real disorder were the immediate outcome of the collapse which may explain the large number of unrecovered hoards. The large number of finds in Somerset suggests localised disturbance of particular intensity, in which those with money felt especially vulnerable. Over the longer term, perhaps the first half of the fifth century, the result was a swift decline of the towns as they ceased to be useful centres of economic activity and a parallel fall in the rural population as the countryside returned to subsistence. It is easy to see the situation as one in which the unnatural towns grafted on to Celtic rural life disappear as the outside support collapses, but that is too simple a view of the mechanism involved. Rather, after almost four centuries of development, an economy in which town and country were parts of the same socio-economic system was totally dislocated by being isolated from the rest of the Empire. A population collapse was the natural consequence of such an event. With markets gone and with the need to produce for the market in order to meet tax demands also gone, landowners probably ceased to cultivate grain on a large scale and turned to animal husbandry. As a result they may have felt less need of large numbers of workers. Even the tenant farmer may have been faced with the same choice. With little or no land of his own and no prospect of finding work in towns, poverty and vagabondage would be the lot of those labourers no longer needed and reproduction rates would fall. All this is of course speculation, but it is more likely as an explanation than to imagine that the population simply turned to subsistence farming and carried on as before. Social relationships, especially where they involve the ownership of land, are remarkably persistent and almost always need violence or coercion to overturn them. Men do not simply turn to farm for themselves when their services are no longer required, they starve if they have no land. Nor do we need to postulate otherwise unknown plagues to account for a population collapse. There are no plague pits outside the declining towns, which would have been the first sites to be visited by the disease. Roman Somerset collapsed and those who survived were those who held on to what they already had, the land.

Rebuilding the countryside 407 – 650 AD

Anyone attempting to write the history of the period from 407 to the end of Celtic, that is Old Welsh, Somerset in the mid-seventh century is faced with the near insuperable problem that we have no written sources. Such accounts as we have for the history of Britain in the fifth and sixth centuries are fragmentary and of dubious quality. The Life of St Germanus, the Bishop of Auxerre, tells of a visit to Britain in 429 to combat the spread of the Pelagian heresy (Thompson 1984). It recounts events in the South-East, including preaching in the countryside, a visit to

St Albans and a bloodless battle against the Saxons. Although there is no reason to doubt the reality of the saint's visit, the Life was written well after his death and was, after all, meant to edify the faithful with an account of a holy life. It must, therefore, conform to certain rules and the miraculous battle was certainly the sort of detail that contemporaries expected to read. It is unlikely that the hagiographer knew anything more about Britain than the bare details of the saint's visit. Gildas alone writes as a near contemporary of the events of the second half of the fifth century and his own times. Publishing his *De Excidio c.* AD 500 (Herren 1990), he is a valuble source for the events of the period immediately before his birth, if we remember that he wrote a moral lesson for his contemporaries, not a work aimed at historical truth (Dumville 1977a). He introduces us to a 'tyrant', identified by later writers as Vortigern. It was Vortigern's foolishness which allowed the English to become established. But we can no longer believe in Hengest and Horsa (not named by Gildas), or in the descriptions of the early battles in the Anglo-Saxon Chronicle, for they are all part of the foundation myth of the English and not to be taken literally (Brooks 1989a).

Gildas's Vortigern is shown as being active in the middle of the fifth century. Even if the story of Hengest and Horsa must be dismissed as an English legend, nevertheless Vortigern seems to have been a leader among the British, perhaps in the south (Dumville 1977a, p. 185, n. 60). The story that he invited the English leaders into Britain to use them against other threats may be a remembrance of an attempt to come to terms with the earliest English settlers by offering them lands to settle on. After a while the trickle of settlers became a flood which could no longer be contained and the English became raiders. Warfare against them continued for some fifty years until the battle of *Mons Badonicus*. Miller (1976) suggests that the battle must have taken place soon after the beginning of the sixth century, but an earlier date for the *De Excidio* must place the battle of Mons Badonicus in the late 450s. This is not inherently improbable if it describes a successful end to a period of violent warfare between the English and the Romano-British. This battle checked the English and produced a peace between the two peoples which was to last for nearly fifty years, although there is no reason to suppose that this meant that piecemeal settlement came to a halt. There is nothing in the historical record which makes King Arthur a real figure here and even less that would connect him with Somerset. All we can say is that by the early years of the sixth century it seems as if a stable regime existed in Somerset which was Celtic and not English, although it may have had some English elements settled in it.

Of all surviving early English place-names 'wickham' (OE **wichām**) has a claim to be the oldest (Gelling 1967). Three such possible place-names survive in Somerset (Fig. 3.2). The first is in the parish of West Camel (ST 582 237), where a field name is unfortunately only available in a modern version (D/D/Rt 118). This site lies equidistant between Cadbury Castle and Ilchester and also close to the road from Wiltshire. The second site was in the parish of Ditcheat, close to the Roman villa site at Laverns and also close to the Lamyatt Beacon pagan temple which had long since ceased to be used as a place of pagan worship. It is also not far off the Fosse Way. Some medieval evidence for this place-name exists. It was *wykhamstyle* in 1308–10 and *wickham ash* in 1842 (Egerton 3321, and D/D/Rt 143). The third site lay in Congresbury, not far from the Wemberham Roman villa and Cadbury-Congresbury hillfort. This **wichām** also has early modern place-name evidence – *wykehamfurlong* in 1475 and in 1500 (DD/T/Ph/VCH 5(i), CR 233 and 234). Such place-names may represent early settlers among the local sub-Roman population, planted on lands deserted by locals. Certainly the 'wichams' are intimately connected with Roman sites. The major objection is to the survival of such names through a period when English was not the language of the district. John Morris argued forcefully for the conquest of the Ilchester area in the mid-sixth century (Morris 1973, pp. 294–6). He relied upon the evidence of pagan burials in the district around Ilchester (Meaney 1964, pp. 218–19). These burials were at Huish Episcopi, Queen Camel, Evercreech and Buckland Dinham (this last is a long way from Ilchester) (Meaney 1964). Re-examination of the burials suggests that the evidence for pagan Saxon burials in the region is far from convincing; for while the first two examples are probably sixth-century burials the second two are very badly recorded and need not be connected with Ilchester, but rather with Shepton Mallet. On balance, even if there were a few early Anglo-Saxon settlers in the area at an early date, there seems little doubt that

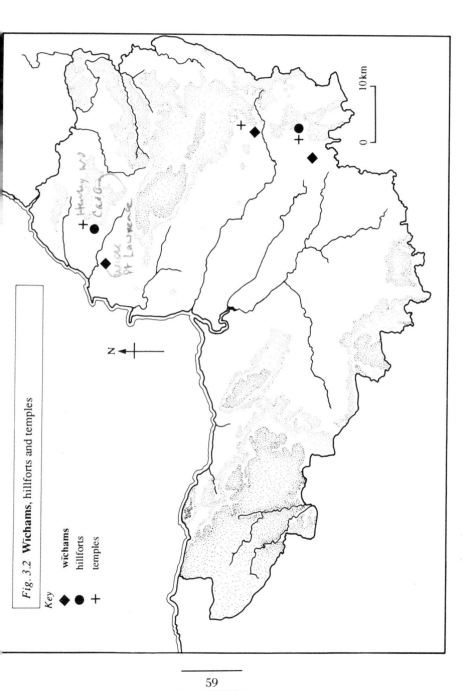

Fig. 3.2 **Wichams**, hillforts and temples

Key

wīchams

hillforts

temples

◆

●

+

N

10 km

0

59

this was a region of Celtic, that is Old Welsh, dominance, in which a well-organised society existed for more than 250 years.

Surviving direct evidence of the Old Welsh society in Somerset is difficult to find. Very little has survived of what must once have been a rich variety of Old Welsh place-names. Although there are many modern names which contain Old Welsh elements, these are almost always the result of an Old English place-name formed by a compound which uses an Old Welsh river name or name of a natural feature, or the result of the settlement being named directly from a river. For example 'Bruton' was formed as an Old English place-name by adding OE **tūn** to the OW **briw**, which was the river name, to form the compound with the meaning of 'the settlement on the river Brue'. No knowlege of Old Welsh would be neccessary to form the name, only knowledge of the name of the river.

Similarly, many names were formed using Old Welsh elements which had been taken into Old English and their use in forming a name does not necessarily denote the survival of an Old Welsh name. Near Taunton there is a hill called Creechbarrow Hill (ST 248 256). The name first appears in a charter of AD 682 (S. 237) recording a grant to Glastonbury. The Latin boundary clause of this charter is probably a compilation made at a date later than the original charter, but still contains material from the seventh century (Edwards 1988, pp. 15–17). In the bounds is a reference to *collem qui dicitur brectannica lingua cructan, apud nos crycbeorh*, 'the hill which is called **cructan** in the British language but among us **crycbeorh**'. Here is a clear statement that two names were subsisting in parallel in the later seventh century: the Old Welsh name and the English name side by side. Moreover the English name contains the very common element **cric** which was borrowed from the Old Welsh **crūc** 'a hill' and which occurs in many modern place names as 'creech'. It is likely that its meaning was understood when it was first borrowed, but later elements such as **beorh** 'a hill' were added as understanding of the Old Welsh element faded. Clearly this point had already been reached by the later part of the seventh century in Somerset. The survival of later Old English place-names which contain Old Welsh elements taken from topographical features is not a sign of the survival or continuity of settlement, but a sign of early Anglo-

Saxon name formation in a landscape where the pre-existing names of rivers and hills survived.

The existence of two names in parallel illustrates the way in which many Old Welsh names must have disappeared in quite a short space of time, as Old English became the dominant language. Some Old Welsh names did persist, but their survival was chance, rather than due to any conscious policy. An example of this is 'Tarnock', near Brent Knoll. The hamlet of Tarnock is inside Biddisham parish. The name, as the name of a stream, occurs in the bounds of the charter of AD 693 AD for the estate at Brent (S. 238), where it is **ternūc**. The same place appears in 946/955 as **tornoc** (Carley 1978, p. 51) and in the probably spurious charter of AD 1065 as *Biddisham quod Tarnock proprie appelatur*, 'Biddisham the proper name of which is Tarnock' (S. 1042 and Liber Albus II, fo. 241–2). This shows the process by which an Old Welsh name was swallowed up by the Old English name, although in this case the usual final disappearance of the first name did not happen.

More significant names are those attached to sites which were of importance in the Old Welsh period. The most obvious example is that of the estate of Brent. Today the name survives as the name of the prominent hill with its Iron Age fort, known as Brent Knoll. Two parishes surrounding the hill are now called East Brent and Brent Knoll, although this last was formerly South Brent. However, the name first appears as that of an estate granted to the abbey of Glastonbury in AD 693 (Edwards 1988, pp. 23–5). The boundary clause of the charter is a simple one, in Latin, which describes a very large block of land. It reads *habens ab occidente sabrinam. ab aquilone Axam. ab oriente ternuc. ab austro siger*, 'having the Severn to the West, to the North the Axe, to the east the Ternuc, to the south the Siger'. These boundaries include the modern parishes of East Brent, Brent Knoll, Lympsham, Berrow and Brean (Fig. 3.3). As we have seen in Chapter two, the name is Old Welsh, and, in this very early charter, belongs to the whole estate, not simply to the hill. A villa site has been recorded at Lakehouse Farm while the possible temple site on the hilltop had burials as well as wall plaster and pottery (Leech 1977, p. 255, fig. 19). The dedication of the parish church at Brean, within the estate has also been

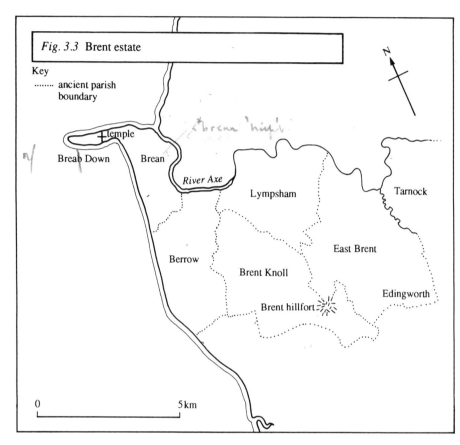

Fig. 3.3 Brent estate

Key

········ ancient parish boundary

N

temple

Breab Down   Brean

River Axe

Lympsham   Tarnock

East Brent

Berrow

Brent Knoll

Edingworth

Brent hillfort

0   5 km

noted. It seems possible that Brent as it appeared in the late seventh century represents the central part of an estate which was simply transferred directly into the ownership of the monastery at Glastonbury and points to the way in which the Old Welsh countryside may have been organised.

A somewhat similar site existed at Cannington. Here at the hillfort it has been demonstrated that there was some form of continuous occupation on the site from late Roman times until the late seventh or the eighth century (Rahtz 1969). Five hundred and twenty-three graves were recovered from a hillside on the east side of the fort, but estimates of the size of the cemetery suggest that there may have been between 2,000 and 5,000 burials. The excavator has quite rightly been extremely cautious in his assessment of the cemetery site and its relationship to the hillfort (Rahtz 1977). However, more recent field work by Ian Burrow has suggested the existence of a post-Roman settlement just outside the walls of the fort (Burrow 1981, pp. 78–80). The cemetery was not therefore isolated on the hilltop, near the hillfort, but part of a settlement pattern. The place-name contains an Old Welsh element of great interest. The early spellings of the name show that it was **cantūctūn** in the ninth century, when named in King Alfred's Will (S. 1507 of 873–88) 'the tun by the Quantocks'. The hills in turn preserve the same element, **cantūc**, perhaps from the British *cantaco, 'a district divided off'. Its transference to the range of hills suggests that it applied at an early date to the whole of the region between the hills and the sea (see Fig. 3.4). The district became a royal estate immediately after the Anglo-Saxon conquest of Somerset (see below). As with the estate at Brent, the early estate pattern may well preserve something of the older Old Welsh pattern. The large cemetery might represent the burial place of the whole estate, in use throughout the Old Welsh period and perhaps well into the Anglo-Saxon period, until the establishment of the church and associated graveyard in Cannington. A parallel elsewhere would be the existence of large Old Welsh estates whose boundaries are preserved in the parishes of Braunton and Hartland in North Devon (Pearce 1985).

At Congresbury, the hillfort of Cadbury-Congresbury has produced evidence of reoccupation in the post-Roman period. Here was found pottery from the Mediterranean, similar to that found at South Cadbury, demonstrating that the site was in use towards the end of the fifth century (Burrow 1981, chap. 6). Imported glass and pottery was clearly high status material. Some of the vessels may have contained wine or oil; other objects were clearly for use by important people (Rahtz 1987). Ian Burrow has attempted a theoretical reconstruction of the possible territory of the hillfort (1981, p. 173). That reconstruction embraces the site of the Yatton Roman villa as well as the **wichām** site mentioned above. The site is closely connected with the nearby Henley Hill pagan temple, and within the possible territory is another dedication to St Bridget, at Chelvey, analogous to the dedication at Brean. The parish, within which the hillfort stands (and the modern settlement) are named after the Celtic saint Cyngar, so

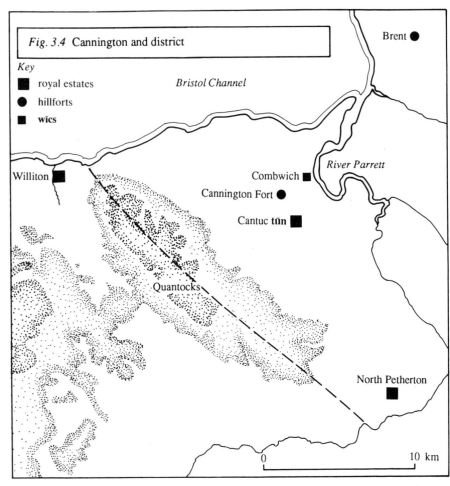

Fig. 3.4 Cannington and district

Key
- ■ royal estates
- ● hillforts
- ■ **wīcs**

Bristol Channel

Brent ●

River Parrett

Williton ■

Combwich ■

Cannington Fort ●

Cantuc tūn ■

Quantocks

North Petherton ■

0   10 km

we cannot dismiss the possibility that a Celtic monastery stood nearby.

At Glastonbury, excavation on the Tor itself yielded traces of wooden buildings on the summit, sherds of imported Mediterranean pottery, together with Roman tile fragments, post-Roman metal objects and evidence of metalworking. The large number of animal bones and the site itself might reasonably be interpreted as indicative of a secular site (Rahtz 1971). If so, this might also be the centre of another of these large estates, one which later emerged as the estate of the monastery at

Glastonbury. On the other hand the excavator has more recently inclined towards explaining the site as an early example of a religious settlement, so that the question must be left open for the moment (Rahtz 1983).

The sites already discussed, such as Cannington, Brent and Congresbury, may each be areas of land controlled by a single family of high status. What we see is probably a territory which has at its centre some focal point which links the estate to its late Roman past. At Cannington the settlement and the graveyard at the hillfort provide the focus. The only known villa site is at Spaxton, within the territory of Cannington, but irrelevant by the later fifth century. At Congresbury a hillfort site was reused, perhaps partly as a defended site, but also as a site which gave some prestige. Here there is a link with the Henley Hill pagan temple site, only a few hundred yards away, with its later, possibly Christian, burials. Within the possible territory of the hillfort lay the abandoned villa at Wemberham in Yatton. Brent estate was built around a disused hillfort with a former temple site and a nearby villa site. If this reconstruction of landholding is close to reality, then it is likely that the whole of later Somerset was organised into large units, perhaps the successors to the territories of the larger villas. The focus for each of these territories may have varied from place to place. Hillforts provide the focus, even if not still occupied and refortified, at Brent, Cannington and Congresbury. At Bruton, on the other hand, the centre was provided by the pagan temple site on the hilltop at Lamyatt Beacon, with the Roman villa of Ditcheat nearby. It seems unlikely that any substantial area of land would be able to resist inclusion in a zone of influence, controlled by some member of the aristocracy. Such a reorganisation probably represented only a shift of focal point and would have come about quite quickly with the loss of central authority, and once established would tend to be stable as long as the social organisation which produced it survived.

We know next to nothing about the interior organisation of these estates. Clearly, those places, such as Tarnock and Winterhead, which still have names of Old Welsh origin, are likely to be estates which have a continuous history from sub-Roman times, although we must be careful to avoid the assumption that the settlement itself has a continuous history.

Such sites are rare, however, and we must look elsewhere for evidence of continuity. The common place-name element **wīc** may provide it.

The Old English **wīc** is an early borrowing from the Latin **vicus**, which had entered the language before the migration to Britain (Smith 1970). By the time that the early English settlers began to meet the word in Latin, in Britain, it had already been generalised to mean nothing more than 'village' (Johnson 1975). Smith points out that as an undeclined plural in Old English, it took the meaning 'village or settlement' and generated many compounds, such as Barwick, near Yeovil, which was *Berewyk* (1315–16) (Dickinson 1889 [Nomina Villarum]). Smith also suggested that the term may not have been in use at an early date, but developed later to produce a wide variety of names in many parts of the country. It can be taken as a term for a variety of minor settlements and single farms.

Professor Ekwall summarised opinion and suggested that the most common meaning of the word was 'dependent farm', though other meanings such as 'dairy farm', 'homestead' and 'port' also existed (Ekwall 1960; 1964). More recently Della Hooke has seen the term as indicative of dairy farming in the valleys of the Teme and the Severn, round about Worcester (Hooke 1981, p. 294). It would be foolish to deny that the English may have used the element in making place-names. However, it is possible that the name is susceptible of other explanations. As an element **wīc** is quite common in Somerset. Sixty-one occurrences have been noted, of which forty-five can be identified today. Some are modern parishes, others are farms or hamlets and some exist only as field-names. They are much more common in the north and east of the county than they are in the west. There is evidence that they are frequently found in association with known Roman villa sites and this can be demonstrated statistically. The mean distance between **wīcs** and villa sites is 3·46 km and the mean distance between a large (134) sample of tun settlements and villa sites is 5·73 km. The difference between the two means was 2·245 km and the standard error of difference was 0·68. There is a less than 1 per cent probability that this difference is random. **Wīc** settlements may be survivals from the sub-Roman pattern. It is not chance that they are concentrated in lowland Somerset, where the majority of the romanised settlement is also found.

The pre-eminent site, which has produced the best evidence for reuse, is Cadbury Castle. Here the work of Professor Leslie Alcock established that it had been refortified in the second half of the fifth century and that it continued to be used into the late sixth century. The scale of the refortification is such that it cannot be compared with any other site in the region. Here was an Iron Age hillfort which had seen some use, at least as a religious site, into the late Roman period and which was refortified so that the 1,200 metre perimeter enclosed eighteen acres of land (Alcock 1972, pp. 174–93). The new rampart used over 20,000 metres of timber (Alcock 1987, p. 195). The scale of the operation needed to harvest and convert this amount of wood clearly demonstrates its importance in the political economy of the region. The presence of a large hall on the hilltop is good evidence of occupation by individuals of high status. This view is reinforced by the presence of imported Mediterranean pottery.

Although we do not need to envisage a defending army of great size, it seems unlikely that Cadbury Castle would have been reoccupied and the walls rebuilt so lavishly unless it was used at some point by military forces. The site looks eastward. It guards the access to Somerset from the south-east and east, acting both as a bulwark against advance from the east and as a dominant site for the central Somerset basin (Fig. 3.5). As such it is the successor to Ilchester as the focal point for commerce and politics in the district. The presence of the imported pottery indicates contacts by sea with western Gaul, though not necessarily trade. This contact may have had political significance, especially where it involved relations with the western part of Gaul, despite the relative distance of the site from the sea. Cadbury Castle was both a military and a political site. Had it been refortified solely as a military strongpoint, the area to be defended could have been considerably reduced. South Cadbury may have had an active life of about a century, to judge by the dating evidence. It was certainly in use throughout the time of the battle of Mons Badonicus and during the period of peace witnessed by Gildas and so strongly supported by most modern commentators. Pagan Old English burials in Wiltshire extended into the western part of the county, to the south of Warminster (Meaney 1964), showing that English settlement had moved up to the Somerset border by c. AD 600 or soon after. The most recent review of the origins

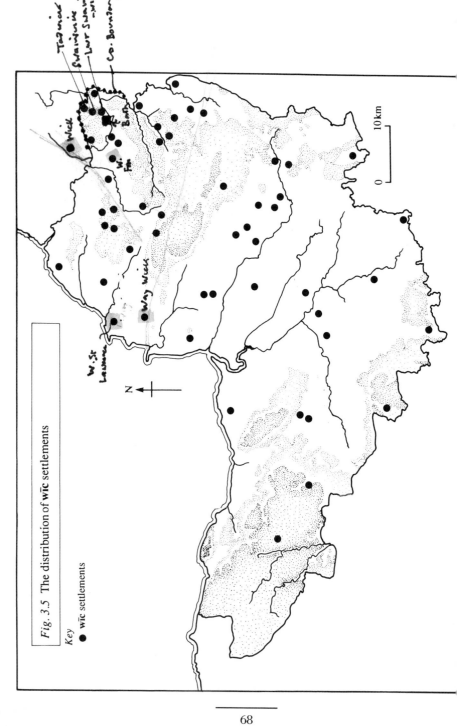

Fig. 3.5 The distribution of **wīc** settlements

Key
● wīc settlements

10km

N

W. St Lawrence

Wey Week

Wick

W. Firle

W. Burn

Tadmead
Swaninwic
Low Stawine-wick
Co. Boundary

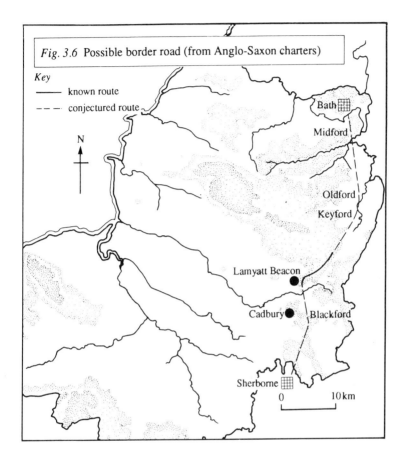

Fig. 3.6 Possible border road (from Anglo-Saxon charters)

Key

—— known route

– – – conjectured route

N

Bath

Midford

Oldford

Keyford

Lamyatt Beacon

Cadbury   Blackford

Sherborne

0   10 km

of the West Saxon kingdom suggests that it came into being as the result of conquest from the Thames Valley area, which was aimed southward (Yorke 1989). The early English around Salisbury were held back by the existence of Cadbury and there is little to suggest that they were expansionist during the fifty years of peace after the battle of Badon. There must have been a border between the English and the Old Welsh. South Cadbury looks towards that border and it may be that the Selwood Forest, extending from Chippenham in the north to Gillingham in the south, and probably running eastward into modern Wiltshire, provided a no-man's land, with the few routes through the woodland easily supervised by the hillfort. North to south there ran a road which certainly came from Sherborne and passed close to the old temple site at Lamyatt Beacon before heading towards Bath in the north. This route is marked by roads and tracks which are evidenced in the later Anglo-Saxon period (see Fig. 3.6), but which clearly predate the establishment of the early English Bruton. It provided a line of communication behind the frontier zone, which, as far as we can tell, lasted until the mid-seventh century.

The re-emergence of a state

At this point we can return to the question of the larger political picture. How was this patchwork of post-Roman estates governed? How far did an organised government exist and how extensive was its authority? We can begin by dismissing King Arthur. We have no evidence for his existence and we do not need to introduce either a *deus ex machina* to explain events in the late fifth and early sixth century or a spurious sense of personality in a period when we do not know the names of more than half a dozen men. Gildas is the only authority we have for political events in the later fifth century and he is exceedingly obscure. It is clear that in his day − the late fifth century − there existed a King of Dumnonia. He was mentioned by Gildas as a tyrant who had murdered two young men of royal status (Winterbottom 1978, 28: 1, 2). Gildas mentioned the deed as an example of tyranny, but it also suggests dynastic instability. Furthermore his private life was castigated by Gildas, who accused him of having put away his lawful wife. He may have had difficulties in getting an heir, or needed a new wife as part of a political alliance. It is likely that these manifestations of wickedness were tied to the same instability which produced civil wars also mentioned by Gildas (Winterbottom 1978, 26: 2).

This king probably had some kind of civil administration available to him, although we should not exaggerate its abilities. Recent research suggests that Gildas himself had been educated by a rhetor so that he was the product of the late Roman system, designed to educate lawyers and administrators for the Roman governmental system. He was not educated as a monk (Lapidge 1984, p. 49). If that education was received in the 470s in anti-

---

70

cipation of a governmental career, there is at least the suggestion that a system existed at that time, into which he might go, or that the demise of the system was recent. It may have ceased to exist in Gildas's lifetime, as the slide into barbarism continued. But at least in the late fifth century there were still men who could think and write in fluent late Latin and there were other men available to read what had been written.

A monarchy with dynastic struggles between members of the ruling family, a civil administration, control of landowners and peasantry and a military capability had fixed boundaries to its territory to the east. South Cadbury policed and guaranteed the boundary in the south-east. To the north it seems likely that the territory of the Dubunni had been absorbed into the region dominated by Cadbury. Here the major 'Dark Age' survival is the Wansdyke. It consists of a bank and ditch, facing north, which runs, with gaps, from Maes Knoll in the west to Bath in the east. The battle of Dyrham, in AD 577 (ASC) marked the loss of north-west Wiltshire and southern Gloucestershire by the Old Welsh. The Anglo-Saxon Chronicle speaks of the defeat of three kings at the three 'cities' captured as a result of the battle. We need to remember that the Anglo-Saxon Chronicle is not a document of record upon which we can rely. The Hwicce in northern Gloucestershire, Worcester and Warwickshire who controlled the south-western part of the Midlands were still British in the seventh century. The Old English involved were probably Gewissae from the Thames valley area, not from south-east Wiltshire, and what they did was to drive a wedge between Welsh Somerset and the Hwicce. It is possible that Wansdyke was constructed as a political boundary between the Old Welsh of Somerset to the south and the new English groups to the north, the Gewissae. It is certainly not a boundary which could ever have been defended by troops. There can be little doubt that the dyke itself predates the English arrival in Somerset and that it is post-Roman (see Fig. 3.7). The name might have been given by the English around Bath in the late seventh century, faced with a feature whose origins were unknown to them. Where the dyke crosses the parishes of Stanton Prior and Marksbury it ignores the estate boundaries which certainly existed in the tenth century (Costen 1983). The estates in the area may be grouped around the hillfort of Stantonbury and the dyke cuts right through this

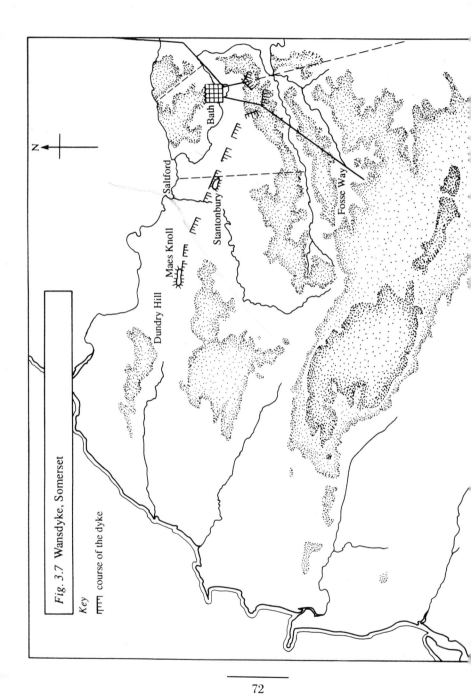

Fig. 3.7 Wansdyke, Somerset

Key

⊤⊤⊤ course of the dyke

Bath

Saltford

Dundry Hill

Maes Knoll

Stantonbury

Fosse Way

N

Why not Roman?

estate. If this is the nucleus of yet another large sub-Roman estate, Wansdyke would certainly postdate it, since it cuts right through the estate, using the hillfort of Stantonbury as part of the line. It is most unlikely that the boundaries of the estates would have been laid out to ignore so prominent a landscape feature. They must predate the dyke. The Stantonbury estate may have been split as the result of a political decision, but this could have been at any time after AD 410. To the east, the dyke does form a boundary for some of the Old English estates around Bath. It also approaches the city very closely, since a part of it ran along the escarpment at the southern side of Prior Park (DD/SE Box 3).

The evidence of the Anglo-Saxon Chronicle hints at the existence of petty kings among the Old Welsh. Whether they existed in northern Dumnonia cannot be known, but the existence of Wansdyke points to some well-defined political authority, even in the last quarter of the sixth century. It seems unlikely that the dyke could have been regarded as a 'Maginot Line', to be literally defended by soldiers. It seems more likely that it was *became* a negotiated treaty line, rather like the later Offa's Dyke in western Mercia. However, we must be careful to recognise that such a view contains much speculation. The view put forward by Sir Cyril and Lady Eileen Fox in 1958 (Fox and Fox 1958) that it represents a pagan English boundary of the early seventh century seems untenable. There is no evidence that the English had yet settled in any numbers to the south of the Wansdyke.

Post-Roman religious life

The post-Roman society which organised itself so well seems to have been fundamentally Christian. No doubt many pagan beliefs related to the nature worship common among the Celtic peoples of western Europe survived among the peasantry. There is some evidence that the temple site at Pagan's Hill in Chew Stoke continued to function as a religious centre into the fifth century and the well was still open and perhaps in use, though not necessarily for religious purposes, in the seventh century (Rahtz and Harris 1958). In addition to the examples of the possible survival of the cult of Bridget at Brean and Chelvey, as well as the importance of sacred wells which bestowed fertility, there are hints of other survivals of the common beliefs, such as the cult of the severed head (Ross 1967, pp. 104–26). It is not difficult to see the story of St Decumanus at Watchet, who died by having his head struck off and has a holy well, as an example of this Celtic pagan cult transferred to a Christian missionary and co-opted by the church. The very fact that the site is now associated with a Celtic Christian saint shows how successful the conversion of the countryside was.

Although there is no certainty about where he came from, or where he was working, the evidence of Gildas in the very early sixth century is an impressive witness to the standing of the church in his society. Dr Nicholas Higham has recently argued for the land of the Durotriges, modern Somerset, Dorset or eastern Wiltshire, as the likely region where Gildas was working (Higham 1991a, forthcoming). Although he saw his society as filled with wicked men, there is no doubt that they were wicked in a Christian context. The deeds of King Constantine of Dumnonia, murderer of royal youths, had a special horror because the crime also involved sacrilege, evidently at a monastery (Winterbottom 1978, 28: 1, 2). Another ruler was accused of falling away from his plan to become a monk (Winterbottom 1978, 34: 1, 2, 3). The continued existence of priests, and bishops, is evidenced for the beginning of the sixth century and it seems unlikely that the organisation of Christianity broke down in those areas not occupied by the pagan English, although the system of bishops in the towns certainly failed (Thomas 1981, p. 267).

However, there are no remains of churches surviving in Somerset from the fifth or the sixth centuries, although the existence of some can be inferred for the later sixth-early seventh century. Evidence for Christian activity must come from other evidence, slightly less direct, the best known of which comes from the survival of graveyards which may be Christian.

Philip Rahtz has examined the known sub-Roman cemeteries, including those in Somerset (1977). His investigation included sites at Camerton, Doulting, Portishead, Wint Hill (Banwell), Brean Down, Henley Wood and Worlebury (Weston-super-Mare), to which can be added Daws Castle, near Watchet (Burrow 1981, p. 87). Rahtz makes the important point that it would be wholly simplistic to assume that these cemeteries are neccessarily Christian, simply because they lack grave goods and are normally oriented east-west. Nevertheless, at Cannington the cemetery was in use from the second century until the seventh or eighth century. It may have contained from 2,000 to 5,000 graves, although only 523 remained to be excavated in 1962. The excavator is very strict in his analysis of the material, insisting that the cemetery may have moved from paganism to Christianity, perhaps in the sixth century, and then have continued into the early English period. Of particular interest was the discovery of the grave of a young woman which seems to have provided a focus for many burials. Her grave was specially marked by a low mound and a setting of imported stone. There was evidence that her grave (radiocarbon dated to AD 621), was frequently visited. The best explanation would be that this was a Christian burial of the 'martyrium' type. The graveyard is clearly important in a number of ways. It shows that continuity of settlement and community was strong enough to survive changes in religious belief; that a cemetery of this size accounted for the population for a considerable area round about; and that religious expression, even when Christian, took place within a context which acknowledged the dominance of the local ruler. If, as suggested above, Cannington was the centre of a great estate, the cemetery would fit neatly into such a scheme.

No other site approaches Cannington in size. At Brean Down the burials were numerous but unquantified. Carbon dates were sixth century and the pagan temple site stood on the hill above the cemetery (Apsimon *et al.* 1961). This might have been the cemetery for the Brent estate, within which Brean Down stood.

At Henley Wood, Yatton, between 50 and 100 graves were placed through the temple building, thus postdating its use, and may have been sixth century. This cemetery may have been linked with the site at Cadbury-Congresbury and thus to the suggested estate. At Lamyatt, the small cemetery of *c.* sixteen graves lay close to the pagan temple and contained burials which were rather loosely oriented and for which radiocarbon dating suggests sixth to eighth century deposition. The excavator has suggested that this may be a Christian cemetery using a known holy site (Leech 1980, p. 349). If so, it would be a cemetery at the centre of another large estate, based initially upon the villa site at Laverns in Ditcheat and the Romano-British settlement site at Sutton nearby.

Dr Roger Leech has also suggested that the hamlet at Bradley Hill, which had a cemetery with forth-six burials, aligned east-west, may be evidence of Christianity in a rural community between the late fourth and the first half of the fifth century. None of the graves showed any sign of grave goods (Leech 1980, p. 345).

At Camerton the cemetery with c. 100 graves is associated with the Romano-British settlement, but has graves which indicate a period of use from the fourth to the seventh centuries (Fowler and Rahtz 1972, p. 200). Fowler and Rahtz suggest that this is evidence of continuity of occupation for Camerton. The present writer would prefer to see it as an example of continuity of use for a traditional and possibly Christian burial site for a district, rather than a particular settlement.

A burial site which may be Christian is also known at Wint Hill, where the extensive cemetery reused a Roman villa site. This may have been because the site had retained Christian associations long after it had fallen into ruin. A parallel might be the siting of the later, English, minster church on the site of the Roman villa at Cheddar.

The site at Portishead, with forty-three graves, was probably late fourth century and later, with its graves oriented east-west (Fowler 1969, p. 51). Was it connected with nearby Portbury? Similarly at Daws Castle, near Watchet, the 'numerous' graves found in the earthwork may be associated with the holy well and later church of St Decuman nearby (Rahtz 1977, p. 61). The saint's well and the cemetery may be the religious centre of an estate which later became the royal estate of Williton.

On Winford Hill, on Exmoor, stands the 'Caractacus Stone' with its dedication to *Carataci nepus*, 'the kinsman of Caratacus'. This is probably a fifth-century Christian memorial and is one of a small group of such stones known in the Somerset and North Devon coastal area (Grinsell 1970, pp. 103–4). Many more of these memorials have survived in other parts of the West of Britain (Thomas 1981, pp. 283–5) and they indicate the existence of a literate and Christian elite, powerful enough to erect public monuments. No survivals of this type are to be found anywhere else in Somerset and although this might be due to the ravages of time, it might equally well represent a real distribution, with lowland Somerset outside the area of such practices in the fifth century.

Such other indications of Christianity as exist are most securely connected with the sixth century. Dedications of churches to Celtic saints of the sixth century have been used to suggest Christian activity, particularly in north and west Somerset (Burrow 1981, p. 164; Rahtz 1982, p. 102). It is difficult to support this view, attractive as it is, in the light of the researches of Dr Susan Pearce. She has suggested that nearly all the dedications can be explained as the result of a resurgence of interest in Celtic saints at Glastonbury in the later eleventh century (Pearce 1973). The only Celtic saint's association left secure is St Congar at Congresbury. To this site can be added the lost church site of Lantocal 'the church of Cai' at Leigh in Street, which is mentioned in a charter of 677–92, (S. 1249 and Edwards 1988, pp. 18–19) and the site of another chapel on the island of Marchey, dedicated to St Martin and after whom the island is named (S. 1253 of AD 712). Such a dedication could be indicative of the influence of northern Gaul on Old Welsh religious life in the sixth and seventh centuries.

These last two churches were the property of Glastonbury Abbey in the early English period but did not belong to the monastery prior to the later seventh century. To suggest that they did would be to admit the existence of Glastonbury as a Celtic monastery. No archaeological evidence exists to link the present site of Glastonbury with the sub-Roman period although Dr C. A. R. Radford has long since propounded the view that Glastonbury was a Celtic monastery (1975; 1981). Professor Carley also seems inclined to accept this view (1988, pp. 2–4), but there is nothing positive to date the *Vetusta Ecclesia* to a pre-English time. Neither need the *vallum* which surrounded it and probably enclosed other buildings in the early monastic complex be Old Welsh (Aston and Burrow 1982, pp. 119–20). On the other hand, it is known that there once existed a charter which was ascribed to an unknown Welsh king, and which granted five hides of land to Glastonbury. William of Malmesbury recited the details of the charter, which does not survive and which was supposedly dated to 601. Current opinion is divided. Dr Edwards has suggested it is authentic, in which case Glastonbury could have been in existence as a monastic site before the mid-sixth century (1988, p. 65). Dr David Dumville is of the opinion that it is not genuine (personal comment). The name of the abbot to whom the grant was made is suspiciously English in its form. Other candidates as Celtic Christian monastic sites are Congresbury and, perhaps, Banwell where the churches were described as monasteries when they were granted to the Welsh ecclesiastic Asser by King Alfred (Keynes and Lapidge 1983, chap. 81), but there is no positive evidence which would take their existence back into the early seventh century.

Finally at Wells it has been established that the later Old English minster developed on the site of what has been interpreted as a late Roman mausoleum. This was an underground tomb chamber, large enough for two coffins and possibly supporting a funerary monument above. Nearby was evidence that there had been domestic occupation in the Roman period (Rodwell 1982). It seems that a holy site existed at an early date, and its use by the early English of the seventh and eighth centuries as a religious site strongly suggests continuity or the memory of use throughout the sub-Roman age.

We cannot confidently conclude that any Celtic monasteries existed in Somerset in the mid-seventh century. The nearest would have been the monastery at Sherborne, known as *Lanprobus*, which was probably associated with Cadbury, the most important political centre in Celtic Somerset. It may well be that the political boundary between Dorset and Somerset had yet to be drawn, so there is nothing inherently unlikely in this conjecture. When Glastonbury was set up by the English it represented a clear rival to the Celtic house, which continued to exist after the conquest.

Conclusions

The fragmentary material we have for the history of Somerset between the end of the Roman period and the coming of the English in the mid-seventh century suggests that the withdrawal of the Imperial administration caused a collapse which was economic and which was accompanied by political and social disruption. In that collapse the linked system of towns and rural communities producing for the market came to a rapid end.

Somerset society emerged from the collapse with a much smaller population, organised around the estates of those leading men who had managed to retain control of their land during a period of disorder. Their new society was challenged by the arrival in southern Britain of numerous barbarian settlers, and the period of warfare which broke out stimulated the appearance of local rulers who created a small local state, based upon part of the old *civitas* units, making its headquarters in the refurbished hillfort at Cadbury Castle, with the prestige of its historic local connections, controlling military and trade routes and with its dependent religious centre at Sherborne close by. This was the crucial political act, since the new rulers had also taken control of the strategic centre of the region.

The new state upset the internal balance of power and caused a series of bloody acts by the new rulers as they struggled to retain control. Such unity as they were able to build was secured by the spread of Christianity throughout the whole society. Their adherence to Christianity, which showed itself in the building of churches and the patronage of monasteries, provided the rulers with a powerful claim to legitimacy, since it linked them with the continental Empire and, when that collapsed, with the continental church which had taken over the mantle of the Emperors.

The Old Welsh state in Somerset was lucky that the heaviest onslaught by the invaders came further to the east. Because of the weakness of the English in Wiltshire after the battle of Badon, they were organised only in small groups which posed relatively little in the way of a threat during the sixth century. Towards the end of the century the government of the previous 150 years began to fall apart, leaving the way open for further attacks from the east by the English now unified into the West Saxon people.

4

The coming of the English

According to the Anglo-Saxon Chronicle the English first entered Somerset in AD 658, when Cenwalh 'fought at Pen(selwood) against the Welsh and drove them in flight as far as the Parret' (ASC). Dr David Dumville has rightly made us very suspicious of the information contained in the early part of the Anglo-Saxon Chronicle (Dumville 1977b) and even where we are dealing with the Chronicle in historical times we need to remember its origins within the later West Saxon polity. It is quite clear that we can no longer rely upon the idea of a Wessex which begins with conquest and settlement in central southern Hampshire and then spreads steadily westward. Wulfhere, the Mercian ruler, had previously granted Wight to the King of Sussex, Aethelwealh, in 661 (ASC; Hinton 1981) and the Isle of Wight did not become part of Wessex until 686 when it was conquered by Caedwalla of Wessex (Yorke 1989, p. 89). The expansion of the West Saxons, away from the Thames Valley and into Hampshire and also westward had begun early in the seventh century but Wessex had not really begun to exist until the conquest of the Jutes. It was Ceawlin who emerged as the first of the kings of Wessex (Yorke 1989, p. 95).

If this analysis of early West Saxon history is correct Cenwalh, who fought against the Welsh of Somerset, should be understood as the ruler of the English of the Thames valley. Wiltshire, with its centre at Wilton, near Old Sarum, was a recent acquisition, probably representing a conquest of a smaller group of well-established English settlers. According to the Anglo-Saxon Chronicle, Penda of Mercia had driven Cenwalh out of Wessex and into exile in East Anglia in 645, because he had repudiated Penda's sister. Such an act must have been a sign of a political rupture with Penda. Also, according to the Chronicle, Cenwalh made grants of land and authority to his kinsmen in the Berkshire region. It may be that these grants were forced out of him and that they represent the price Cenwalh paid for his defiance of Penda. Cenwalh also became a Christian in the first year of his exile, 646, and this change of belief is probably connected with the political crisis he was suffering. Christianity had already been introduced to Dorchester-on-Thames in 634, so a change of religious allegiance by Cenwalh would have bought the support of the church in his defiance of Penda. The battle at Bradford-on-Avon in western Wiltshire, in 652, may well have been against other English, perhaps Mercians, rather than against the Welsh. It is doubtful if Cenwalh won the battle. It was Penda's death in 655 and the period before Wulfhere established his authority that gave Cenwalh the opportunity to expand into Somerset.

The Chronicle for 658 says that Cenwalh fought against the Welsh *aet Peonnum* 'at Pen'. The traditional identification of this battle is at Penselwood, on the borders of Wiltshire, Somerset and Dorset, although Professor Finberg suggested that this was actually a site in Devon, Pinhoe near Exeter, and that the conquest took place from the south (1974, p. 31). Sea-borne landings do not, however, seem inherently likely and, moreover, the form of the place-name given in the Anglo-Saxon Chronicle is unequivocal; it cannot have led to the English place-name 'Pinhoe'. A more direct approach from the east, overland, is more plausible. The 'Pen' of the battle would then be somewhere in the eastern part of Somerset, perhaps at Penselwood or some other 'pen' site, such as Penn Hill, just outside Yeovil. Such a site would fit well with the idea that the invaders were anxious to win a political victory and, therefore, directed their attack at the political heart of the Celtic kingdom in east Dumnonia, which was the Ilchester, Somerton, Cadbury area. The Welsh fled as far as the River Parrett, suggesting that the English immediately controlled Somerset as far west as the Parrett-Tone line. The subsequent conquest of the Exeter region then depends upon

D

the identification of Posentesburh with Posbury and with the assumption that Cenwalh won the battle.

All this may be true, but we have no way of assessing the veracity of the Chronicle. For the moment, even the traditional date for the battle of *aet Poennan*, 658, must be regarded with reserve. All we can say is that the surviving charters of the West Saxons reveal the transfer of estates by West Saxon kings and bishops in the last twenty years of the seventh century. One grant to the abbey of Glastonbury, probably made in 681, gave it land at West Pennard (S. 326) and a charter of the following year granted land at Creechbarrow Hill, just outside Taunton and on the slopes of the Quantocks, where a tract of woodland was given (S. 237; Edwards 1988, pp. 11–15) (see Fig. 4.1). The Tone had been crossed and it seems probable that the whole of West Somerset was under English control by this time. How far to the north the West Saxons' rule in Somerset extended is another matter. Quite clearly Bath was not part of Wessex. The charter of 676, which has been accepted as a foundation charter for Bath Abbey, is almost certainly a forgery (S. 51; Edwards 1988, pp. 218–23), and the earliest genuine charter which survives for the abbey at Bath, of the second half of the eighth century, is Mercian (S. 265). There is some place-name evidence that Mercian influence was strong in the region at the time when some place-names were formed. Kelston, just to the west of Bath, on the north side of the Avon preserves a Mercian form in its first element, OE **cēalf**, 'a calf', with its hard initial consonant, as opposed to the expected soft sound of West Saxon. In addition, the place name Publow, OE **pybban hlæw**, 'Pybba's (burial) mound' may well contain reference to a personal name popular in Mercia in the early seventh century (Brooks 1989b, pp. 166–7). This place lies some miles south of the river Avon and, especially if it were a pagan burial, might reflect an English settlement inside Celtic Somerset, which predated the later seventh century West Saxon conquest, or later Mercian infiltration. However, the Avon itself essentially formed the boundary between the West Saxons and the Mercians, since other place-names, such as Chelwood, to the south of Bath, seem to be West Saxon.

We know very little about the internal politics of the early years of the new English province. The charter already quoted shows that Somerset had its own 'king' in the very earliest period.

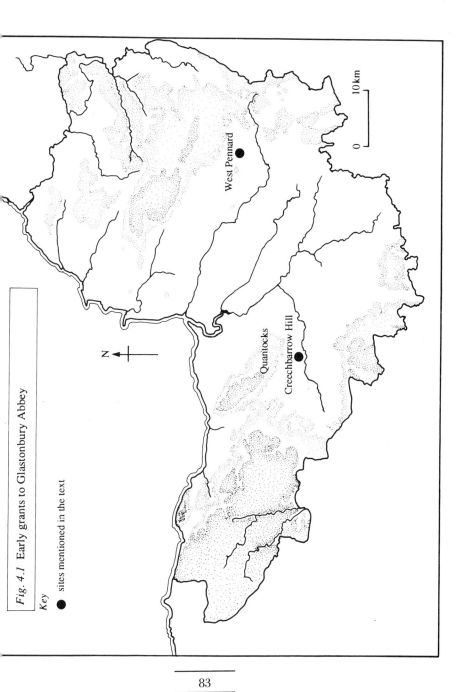

Fig. 4.1 Early grants to Glastonbury Abbey

Key

● sites mentioned in the text

West Pennard

Quantocks

Creechbarrow Hill

N

0 ——— 10 km

Baldred who granted land to Glastonbury in 681 (S. 236) was described in the charter as *Baldredus rex* at a time when Centwine was the King of Wessex (*c.* 676–*c.* 686) so Baldred was a sub-king, probably a member of the royal house. The next charter, nominally dated to the following year, is attributed to Centwine himself (S. 237). The right of succession among early English kings was far from settled, except that it probably belonged to a particular kindred. When Cenwalh died in 672 Bede claimed that the rule was divided between his underkings, but the Anglo-Saxon Chronicle says that Cenwalh's wife, Seaxburh, succeeded him and ruled for a year before being succeeded by Aescwine. The truth is probably that there was a period of weakness, no doubt encouraged by the Mercians, when no one member of the ruling family was actually powerful enough to exert full authority. The political history of Wessex, as detailed in the Anglo-Saxon Chronicle shows that members of the royal family could revolt and rule independently as Caedwalla did from 682 until 688, when the new king Ine drove him out of Britain. In 722 the Queen Aethelburh destroyed Taunton, suggesting that a civil war was in progress in which the Queen was fighting King Ine. Ealdberht, a prince who was probably involved, then fled to Sussex but was pursued relentlessly by Ine and finally killed there in 725. The reign of Ine's successor Aethelheard (728–41) was also marked by war, during which Aethelbald of Mercia captured Somerton in 733. Between the death of Cenwalh in 672 and the accession of Aethelwulf in 839, no son succeeded his father as king of Wessex (Loyn 1984, pp. 15–16). The fragility of political life is in part explained by the lack of any mechanism to ensure quiet succession. Throughout a very long period in the seventh and the eighth centuries the West Saxons were building a society in which a stable hierarchy of government emerged from a loose confederation of chieftains. It is likely that the aggressive urge to expand sprang from the instability of the kin-group. The leading king showed his superiority by leading expansionary and aggressive wars, which provided his loyal followers with land, provided the means to satisfy other members of the kin-group with sub-kingdoms to rule, and added to the wealth of the king himself. There is little evidence to suggest that the expansion was driven by economic needs such as land-hunger by a peasantry, rather it was an aristocratic expansion, driven by political exigencies (Hodges and Moreland 1988).[1] The advent of Christianity at a time when political manoeuvrings were intensifying probably added to the bitterness with which feuds were pursued, since the new religion brought the English into contact with continental models of Christian monarchy which were more highly developed than their own and because the prestigious new missionaries provided the developing kingdoms with religious sanction and support. It is probable that the ideology of Christianity with its strong emphasis on the idea of kingship helped to raise the status of kings and at the same time sharpened the divisions within ruling kin-groups as their leading member was marked out as different and separate from the group.

During this time Wessex was dominated by the power of Mercia, as it largely continued to be throughout the eighth century. The westward expansion, which of course continued into Devon after Somerset had been conquered, must have been sanctioned by the Mercians and would also have acted as an outlet for the needs of the West Saxon aristocracy to find booty and to extend their lands.

The very large territorial unit which the West Saxons were building could only be controlled as a loose confederation, within which pre-existing and new territorial groupings were utilised. Somerset, with its sub-regulus, was one of the new units, the boundaries of which were probably becoming fixed during the second half of the seventh century. As we have seen, the grant of land to Glastonbury which was made in 682 (S. 237) was of land around Taunton and on the eastern edge of the Quantocks. This may reflect recent consolidation of English rule in the area, at a time when land grants were being made to the church. Boundaries with Devon probably depended upon negotiation between an English ruler (a kinsman) at Exeter and the sub-regulus for Somerset and something similar may have happened for Dorset. The village of Rimpton takes its name from being at the edge (OE **rima**) of the county and so probably postdates the

---

[1] Hodges and Moreland (1988) write about a slightly later period of English politics and their analysis of the structure and the forces at work in Middle Saxon England is far more detailed than this study can hope to be. Nevertheless I think that their comments about the importance of ideology and politics probably hold for an early and smaller-scale period.

boundary itself, as does Ryme in Dorset, which lay near the boundary, close to Yeovil (Ekwall 1960). It is likely that these places were named soon after the English arrived, certainly not later than the late seventh century, suggesting that the boundary was established very soon after the English conquest.

Somerset takes its modern name from the *sumortun saete* 'the dwellers around Somerton' (Ekwall 1960) and was first mentioned by Asser in his life of Alfred (Keynes and Lapidge 1983, p. 83), although it was probably current long before Alfred's time. The fact that the shire was to take its name from a royal vill, and that it was an ancient name is of great importance. Somerton is close to the site of Ilchester, which the English recognised as a Roman town, even though it had ceased to be used and its original name forgotten, and it was not far from Cadbury Castle and well placed to use the surviving Roman communications. It was close to the political heart of the new province and yet well connected to centres of power further east in Wiltshire. Although it would be anachronistic to talk of a 'capital', Somerton clearly came to fill a special place in the organisation of the region, since it was mentioned as a place captured by Aethelbald, the Mercian king, in 733. However, it was only one of several major vills in the county which were royal property and which formed the organisational core upon which social and political administration was based.

It would be absurd to suggest that the English failed to utilise the pre-existing structure which they found. To assume that would be to assume that the conquest was attended by mass destruction of the Welsh or their expulsion from the region and an immigrant English population large enough and ready to commence colonisation *ab initio*. This was not a colonisation by settlers of the nineteenth-century type, with an advanced technology and a desire to wipe out the 'natives'. The Laws of Ine, produced some fifty years after the conquest, show that Welsh society continued to exist alongside the new English society, with its structure integrated and apparently still functioning in part. Welshmen owned land: 'A welshman, if he has five hides, is a man of six-hundred wergild' (24.2), 'a welsh rent-payer [has a wergild of] 120 shillings, his son 100: a slave [is to be paid for with] 60, some with 50; a Welshman's hide with 12 [shillings]' (23.3), 'If a Welshman has a hide of land, his wergild is 120 shillings; if however he has half a hide, 80 shillings; if he has none, 60 shillings' (32) (Whitelock 1979, pp. 398–407; the numbers in parentheses refer to the chapter numbers in Ine's Laws). It is just possible, though not proven, that some of the places called 'Walton' may contain reference to Welshmen, OE **Wealh**. These tuns may have belonged to Welsh landholders of the type mentioned in Ine's Laws.

Some outline of the nature of sub-Roman estates in Somerset has been given above. It was those estates which the English incomers found and exploited in the mid-seventh century. The work of G. R. J. Jones on multiple estates and early settlement has been extremely influential in providing a model for the medium-scale organisation of the Old English landscape (1979). The thesis is that late Welsh organisation of the landscape depended upon the existence of large territories, often running to tens of thousands of acres, which were organised on a large scale as integrated units, and which involved economic, jurisdictional and political relationships. Such a unit, typically, had a king as its head and involved a complicated series of relationships between many ranks of people on the estate. Jones's model is based upon rather late, post-Norman Conquest, Welsh Law books. He has, however, convincingly argued for the existence of similar units in the pre-Conquest period outside Wales, in Northumbria and in Kent. More recently, Gregson has criticised the model on the grounds of imprecision and has proposed a systematised model of her own, which provides a discipline upon descriptive efforts (Gregson 1985).

In Somerset the pattern of early place-name material has not hitherto been well understood, but it provides one approach to a problem for which there is little other evidence. Using the multiple estate model, it is possible to place many place-names in a system which explains their existence in the landscape and localises the estate pattern in the county.

There are a very few place-names which are quite simple, but which are associated with major settlements. They usually combine the name of a river with the OE element **tūn** (Campbell 1979, pp. 48–50). The names 'Bruton', 'Taunton', 'Williton', 'Wincanton', 'Chewton', 'Ilton', 'Yeovilton', 'Wrington', 'Petherton' and 'Camerton' are of this type. In 1066 Bruton, Williton, and the two Pethertons, North and South, were royal property (DB 1) (Fig. 4.2). Furthermore, they were all of 'ancient demesne', that is they had been royal property for so long that they had never been rated to the geld and were consequently unhidated. Unfortunately few of these places have independent evidence of their existence prior to the eleventh century. Bruton is mentioned in William of Malmesbury's *Vita* of St Aldhelm (Hamilton 1870) as existing before 705, but we cannot be sure how much of William's topographical information was influenced by tenth-century and contemporary information available to him. Only Taunton is certainly mentioned in the Anglo-Saxon Chronicle in 722. Cannington and Chewton both appear in King Alfred's Will, made between 872 and 888 (Whitelock 1979b, no. 96). It seems overly cautious however, to deny the existence of these royal sites before 700. It seems probable that like Somerton, mentioned in the Chronicle in 733, these places were among the first of the royal settlements in Somerset and that they date from the earliest phase of English occupation. As such they were not villages, but royal centres, probably a hall and accompanying service buildings, surrounded by a palisade, or bank. Even at the time of the Domesday Survey the royal manors which survived were still among the largest estates in the county. At that time Bruton had land for 50 ploughs, North Petherton for 30 and South Petherton for 28. Where estates with these simple names were not royal property at the time of the Norman Conquest there is often reason for believing that they had been part of the royal fisc at an earlier date. Chewton (Mendip) had been King Alfred's property in the later ninth century and then passed by his will to Edward the Elder. Later it became part of the lands of Queen Edith in the time of King Edward the Confessor (DB 1, 29) and had been rated to the geld, but the fact that the Queen held it suggests that it was royal land which was customarily alienated as the Queen's dower. Ilton formed part of the lands of the monastery of Muchelney and was probably granted in the later seventh century, when the monastery was founded. Only Yeovilton, near Ilchester, and Camerton, on the road to Bath, seem to be outside this pattern.

Other simple topographical names also show this pattern of early royal ownership. Thus Cannington, which was discussed above, Somerton, which still had fifty hides in 1086, Carhampton

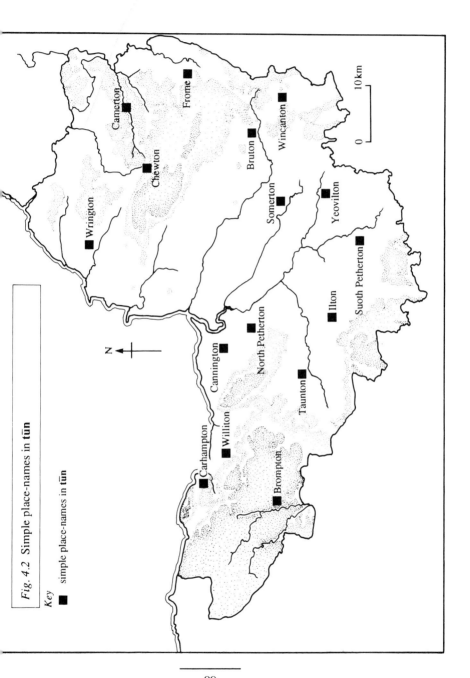

Fig. 4.2 Simple place-names in tūn

Key

■ simple place-names in tūn

and Wrington fit into the scheme. So too does Frome (a simple OW river name, which might easily have become Frampton). Brent was an early royal estate granted to Glastonbury.

Some of these estates can be associated with earlier Old Welsh estates, and are clearly successors to them. Thus Cannington may represent the English royal centre which succeeded the nearby hillfort site. It became the new centre of the English estate, which remained in the hands of the kings of Wessex and then the kings of the English until the Norman Conquest. At Bruton the royal centre lies just below the eastern side of the ancient temple hilltop site of Lamyatt Beacon, with the Roman villa at Laverns in Ditcheat, on the western side of the hill (Fig. 4.3).

These are only two examples, but it seems likely that the general pattern of conquest was that the English kings took over the estates of the previous Old Welsh ruler of Wessex and probably those of many of the chief nobles who could not come to an accommodation with him. He kept the best and largest estates for himself and distributed others to members of the royal kin and to other followers. Once the transfer of land was complete grants to the church began.

Other place-name evidence and some charter grants strengthen the hypothesis that the early English landscape was divided into these large multiple estates and some groups of place-names can best be explained in relation to their central places. Hornblotton, a five-hide estate about 8 km to the west of Bruton has a name formed from the OE **hornblawera tūn**, 'the tun of the horn-blower' (Ekwall 1960) (Fig. 4.3). It seems unlikely that this was a personal name or even a nickname and the best explanation would be that Hornblotton was the estate granted to the man who led the king's hunt. Most of the later royal forest of Selwood lay in Bruton, and in the seventh century a large part of the estate would have been woodland. This place-name is unique in Somerset – although Bemerton in Wiltshire is a close analogy, meaning the 'trumpeter's tun' – but other 'status' names are not uncommon. There are many examples of Charlton – 'the tun of the ceorls' which were probably estates allocated to groups of ceorls (free peasant farmers), who depended directly on the king, rather than on some other lord. They probably paid tribute directly to him and typically these settlements are close to central places (Hooke 1989, p. 13), as for instance at Charlton near

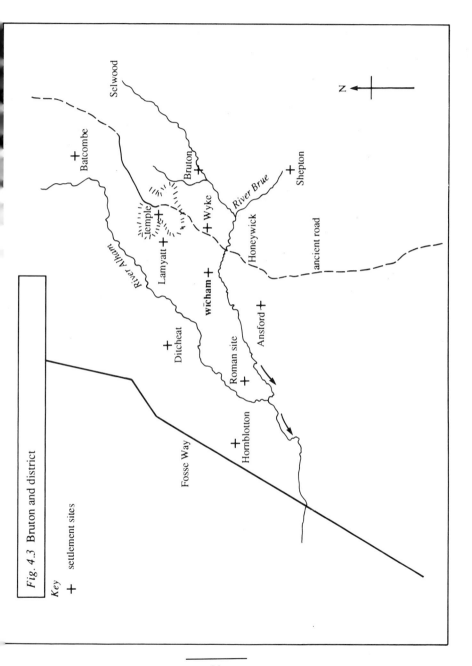

Fig. 4.3 Bruton and district

Key
+ settlement sites

Selwood

Batcombe +

Bruton +

Shepton +

River Brue

Temple

Lamyatt +   Wyke +

Honeywick

River Alham

wīcham +

ancient road

Ditcheat +

Ansford +

Roman site +

Fosse Way

Hornblotton +

N

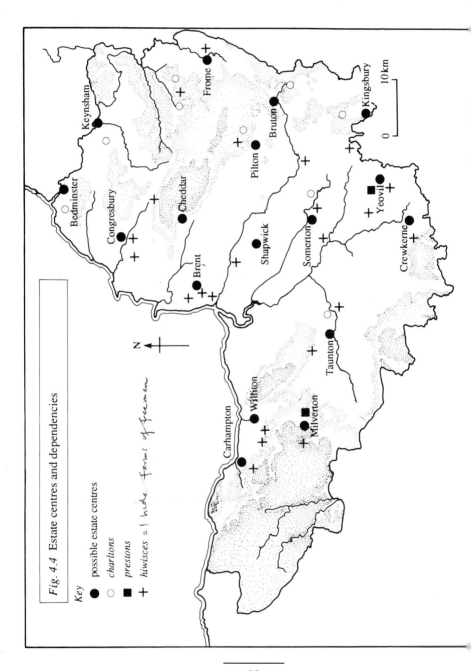

Fig. 4.4 Estate centres and dependencies

Key

● possible estate centres

○ *charltons*

■ *prestons*

+ *hiwisces = 1 hide farms of freemen*

Kingsbury

Frome

Keynsham

Bruton

Pilton

Yeovil

Bedminster

Congresbury

Cheddar

Shapwick

Somerton

Crewkerne

Brent

Carhampton

Wiveton

Taunton

Milverton

N

10 km

0

92

Taunton and Charlton Horethorne, near Kingsbury Regis (Milborne Port) (Fig. 4.4). The Prestons, Prescotts, Prestows and Prestwicks suggest estates granted to priests in return for their services. Chilton Cantelo and Chilton Trinity both preserve OE **cild**, 'a young man', often used in the sense of a 'noble young man'. Here the estate may have been set aside for the support of the lord's eldest son. Athelney, OE **aetheling + ieg**, 'the island of the prince', was royal property until granted to the new monastery by King Alfred. Of all 'status' names Kingstons are probably the most common. These may be settlements which were exploited directly by the king, or which payed rents directly to him.

The 'status' name Kingsbury occurs twice in Somerset, at Kingsbury Regis and Kingsbury Episcopi. In both cases the **burh** of the king may represent the central place on a multiple estate. This is likely to be the case at Kingsbury Regis, in Milborne Port, which was part of a royal estate in 1066 (DB 1, 10).

Other names indicate the use to which a particular estate was put. The 'sheptons' OE **sceap tūn**, 'sheep tun' were estates which specialised in rearing the sheep of the multiple estate, while 'Shipham', OE **sceap + hamm**, 'sheep enclosure', provided the gathering point for sheep from the Mendips, possibly for the king's estate at Cheddar. Calf rearing provided the name for Chelvey, OE **cealf + wīc**, 'calf wic' and Honeywick near Bruton supplied the king's sweetener.

In addition to the estates which were allocated to a specific use and which are identifiable through their names, there were many others which may have had a place in such a pattern but have topographical names or have changed their names over the centuries, as use changed. Place-names which include the element **cott** or **wyrth** record relatively humble settlements. Both are frequently compounded with a personal name, which was probably that of an early tenant. In origin they were probably individual small farmsteads. This is particularly the case for **wyrth** settlements. The term was in use in the seventh century, where it is found in documents but is absent from literary sources and was a word which suggested enclosure (Smith 1970). The many **wyrth** names scattered across the county, some as modern parishes, many others as individual hamlets and farmsteads, probably bear witness to many small individual farmsteads which existed in the seventh and the eighth centuries. Also at a low level of organisation can be found some remnants of the individual farmsteads which probably constituted the holdings of free peasants, the one hide unit or **hiwisc**. /_hwɪʃ_'

This place-name is restricted almost entirely to the south-west of Britain, occurring most frequently in Somerset. Etymologically it is connected with OE **hid**, 'a hide of land', and through a common root to **higan**, 'a family' (Smith 1970). Thus **hiwisc** can be considered to mean 'the land for the support of a family'. As a word it had no currency after the Norman Conquest (Kurath and Kuhn 1952) and does not seem to have been used in coining names in the post-Conquest period. There are twenty-one known **hiwisc** settlements in Somerset (Costen 1992, forthcoming). Some exist as modern parishes, some as hamlets or farms and some are now lost as settlements (Fig 4.4). A few of these estates can still be reconstructed. This is the case at Lovington, Rimpton, Beggearn Huish and Lodhuish. Each **hiwisc** seems to have been a discrete estate which was physically recognisable as a unit, the size of which varied from *c.* 90 ha at Lovington, to 161 ha at Beggearn Huish and 586 ha at Rodhuish. The size seems to have been dependent upon the quality of the land, so that the smaller holdings are to be found in the east of the county where the soil quality is high, while the large **hiwisces** are in the west on high ground, where much of the land was only rough grazing until recently. ·

Some of the **hiwisc** sites which can be identified now have their lands lying in two later manors. This is certainly the case for Cushuish, which was a detached portion of the parish of Kingston St Mary and was made up from two detached portions of the manors of Cothelstone and Kingstone. That they had once been a single unit is shown by the fact that all this land lay within the tithing of Cushuish (Hunt 1962). At Somerton, the **hiwisc** is divided between Somerton and Kingsdon and the same seems to be true of the **hiwisc** at West Hatch, where part of the estate was in Thornfalcon. These examples would suggest that these **hiwisc** settlements were older in origin than the boundaries which now divide them.

In some other cases the **hiwisc** settlement seems to have grown and to have absorbed other units. This is the case at Huish Champflower, where some of the other units, Brown, Middleton and Stolford are still recognisable and at Huish Episcopi where the estate seems to have grown by absorbing the manors of Wearne, Pibsbury and Higher and Lower Bowden.

Although discrete **hiwisc** settlements now only survive in the west of Somerset, it seems clear that they once existed as distinguishable units all over the county. There is some evidence to show that where they have disappeared as units it is because they have become engulfed in the expansion of open-field systems, suggesting that they predate the spread of that type of agriculture. Where they survive intact, as they do at Beggearn Huish and Huish Barton, this is probably because the open-field system never became universal in the hillier and more broken landscapes of West Somerset. **Hiwisces** thus predate the open-field systems of the tenth century and are a survival of an older landscape, in which they were only one type of agricultural element, inside the multiple estate. They are units which probably date from the seventh century and may have origins which predate the Anglo-Saxon settlement of the region, despite their purely Anglo-Saxon name.

The very large number of place-names which reflect small settlements, such as **cott** and **wyrth** as well as the existence of 'use' and 'status' names all indicate a high level of settlement in the county at an early date. In the few cases where early charters have bounds given, as for instance at Shapwick and at Brent (S. 253; S. 238), they embrace very large areas of land. Both these early estates were surrounded by marsh, but this was not regarded as useless and was already apportioned between estates. It is likely that the landscape was fully occupied and that truly waste or unused land was very rare. Perhaps only the tops of the Brendon Hills and Exmoor were really wild, and even here there were probably extensive sheep ranges belonging to the settlements in the combes and valleys.

Woodland existed in some quantity and later evidence suggests that Somerset had been a well-wooded shire. By 1086 only about 11 per cent of the total area of Somerset was wooded and this was only about twice as much as existed in the county in the late Victorian period (Rackham 1980). In 1086 some 70 per cent of all Somerset manors recorded in the Domesday Book had woodland and the median size for woods was about 35 acres. Modern six-inch maps have 970 examples of place-names associated with woodland, **wudu**, **bearu**, **graf**, **hyrst** and **holt**. This suggests that woodland was widely dispersed, but not very great in extent for each settlement. It also suggests that woodland had once been more abundant than it was in 1086. Some large tracts of woodland certainly existed. Neroche forest had much wider bounds than appear in the later Middle Ages. The **stretmerch** of the Muchelney charter, S. 240, is probably part of Broadway parish and part of the forest. On the western side of Neroche the charter for Pitminster, S. 440 of 938 includes a refererence to **wealdenes weg**, 'the forest road', which ran into Neroche. The charter for Creech St Michael, S. 237, has bounds which include *viginti tres mansiones in loco iuxta silva famosam qui dicitur cantucwudu*. The 'well known wood' probably covered the eastern end of the Quantocks. The nearby settlements at Cheddon Fitzpaine (*Ubcedene* and *Succedene* in the Domesday Book) have names from the British *ceto, 'a woodland', suggesting they were close to the forest or within it. The forest of Selwood, which extended along the border between Somerset and Wiltshire was described as *Coit Maur*, 'the great wood', by Asser at the end of the ninth century (Keynes and Lapidge 1983, p. 84). Even as late as 1086 approximately 9,000 acres of woodland within Selwood belonged to the royal manor of Bruton.

Other early concentrations of woodland can be estimated from the modern distribution of place names. The element **lēah** meaning an enclosed woodland or a clearing in woodland (Smith 1970) is widely spread in Somerset. An examination of the region between Ilchester and Wells shows that the element is widespread and that it is early. Settlements which had no woodland in the Domesday Survey have minor 'ley' place-names, showing that they once had woodland. Areas of dense woodland in Selwoood Forest do not always have 'ley' names and they occur frequently across settlements with large and small areas of woodland. The conclusion must be that the element maps woodland in a landscape which had changed dramatically by the end of the Old English period. Distribution of the occurrence of the element on modern six-inch maps (Fig. 4.5) shows concentrations around the edges of the county, but also reveals large areas of woodland near Bath, where the steep valleys probably aided its retention, around the edges of Exmoor and the Quantocks and of course, in the regions known to be forested, such as Selwood and Neroche.

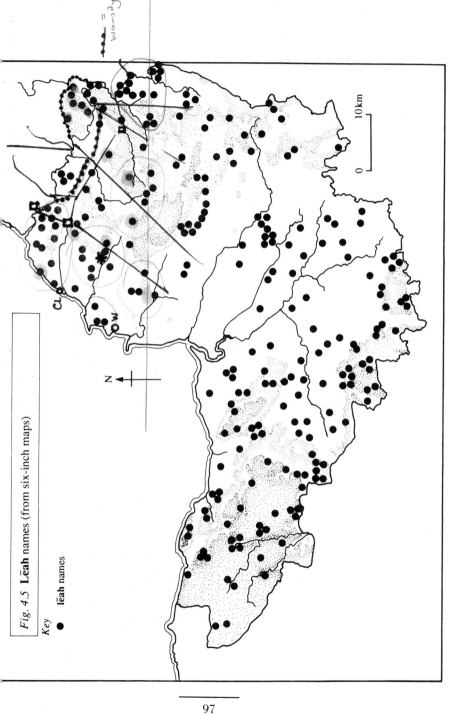

Fig. 4.5 **Lēah** names (from six-inch maps)

Key

● lēah names

Something of a surprise is the area in the north-east of the shire between Banwell and the river Avon. A considerable forest existed there. Selwood Forest itself stretched further westward than it did in the late Old English period, almost reaching Wells. Along the south-facing slopes of the Mendips woodland was common and it is no accident that some of the best preserved areas of ancient woodland are at Cheddar, in just such a situation. Only in the lowland heart of the county was woodland scarce, simply because natural conditions inhibited its growth.

How quickly settlement expanded into the woodlands is impossible to tell. By the tenth century, when the evidence of numerous charter bounds becomes available, woodland was common, but almost always well preserved and cultivated, suggesting that clearance was complete. We should be careful, however, to avoid the suggestion that the early English were settlers dealing with virgin conditions. Ine's Laws, which carefully regulate the preservation of woodland (Whitelock 1979b), may have been enacted with Hampshire or Wiltshire in mind, but they do suggest that regulation of woodland in order to preserve it was already a necessity in the early eighth century. Nothing could be further from the truth than the often repeated story of the early medieval period as one in which peasant huts represented oases of clearance in a wilderness of woodland. The advent of the English probably stimulated population growth and hence the expansion of cultivation within the framework of the existing settlement pattern, but this was from a base of widespread settlement and cultivation.

Even at this early date there was a clear division between east and west Somerset. Royal estates were concentrated in the lowland regions, particularly in the east of the county, in the area most heavily settled in Roman times. Where estates existed in the far west they had their centres on the coastal belt, as was the case for both Williton and Carhampton. This latter probably existed as a royal centre near the seaside and a series of isolated farmsteads and hamlets on the Brendon Hills and Exmoor and this still shows in the tithe map of the parish, with other settlements intruded between parts of Carhampton, where they expanded at a later date (D/D/Rt 277) (Fig. 4.6).

The king's burh was not simply a dwelling place. In Old English society, as Ine's Laws show, the king received tribute and

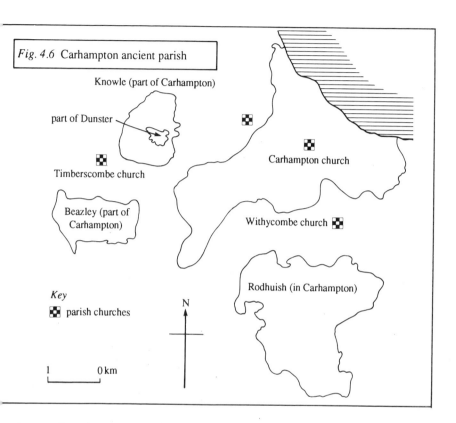

Fig. 4.6 Carhampton ancient parish

Knowle (part of Carhampton)

part of Dunster

Carhampton church

Timberscombe church

Beazley (part of
Carhampton)

Withycombe church

Rodhuish (in Carhampton)

Key

parish churches

N

1   0 km

was also the centre of a system of redistribution (Whitelock 1979b). Hodges has suggested that the redistributive effect of the tribute demanded by Ine was relatively gentle (1982, pp. 136–7). He suggests that the population of a ten-hide unit need have been no more than about twenty-five able-bodied persons to gather the harvest and cultivate the rest of the land. The surplus available would be formidable. I would estimate in a slightly different way, allowing the average hide to support a family of five persons (Herlihy 1985, pp. 68–72), but expecting the ten hides to support a lord and his family of ten people at four times the rate of a peasant household. Allowing the **ceorl** on the hide to cultivate 60 acres would produce a theoretical return of 18 tons (imperial measure) of grain. Allowing one-third for seed would give an output of 12 tons as surplus of which the peasant household might need just over 2 tons. The lord's share might be just under

1·5 tons. The surplus would be very substantial. The problem is that there would be little incentive for the peasant to produce that much grain, since it would be unsaleable. In addition, by no means all farmers were the proprietors of a hide. It is likely that many peasant farms, the **wyrths**, were considerably smaller. Neither is it likely that the theoretical output per acre could ever be achieved. Even so, with the addition of animals the peasant farmer could probably enjoy a comfortable living, even after paying his tithes. His hide could support a larger number of people if he owned slaves to help with his work, as he may well have done.

The king, with his own fisc as well as the tribute laid down in Ine's Laws, could clearly afford to support a substantial group of noblemen at his court and still be in a postion to accumulate and exchange wealth. In Somerset, the king's vill at Somerton was at the centre of exchange. Ilchester/Somerton lies at the centre of a web of communications which runs eastward into Wiltshire and it also controls distribution into Somerset. On the seaward side of the county, the port at Combwich may have functioned much like 'Hamwih' in Hampshire or other 'wic' ports in eastern England, trading with western Gaul, south Wales and Ireland. Cannington would have provided the royal centre to control distribution. In the north, although early Somerset did not include Bath, the route which crossed the Avon at Saltford probably carried salt into the area, running past Stantonbury and southwards towards Camerton (Costen 1983).

Monasteries and churches

The English came into Somerset as Christians and, in the early kings, they had rulers who were often overtly devout. Centwine (*c.* 676/8–685) abandoned the kingdom in order to enter a monastery; Caedwalla, his successor, went to Rome as a pilgrim and died there in 689, and Ine also travelled there after abdicating in 726 (Stancliffe 1983, pp. 155–6). But it is by no means certain that all their subjects were firm believers and there is some evidence for the continuation of pagan practices. The place-name 'Batcombe' occurs twice in Somerset, once near Bruton and again near Cheddar and it also occurs in west Dorset. All three names contain the element **bata**, explained as an OE male name **Bata** (Ekwall 1960). However, the coincidence of the same man's name twice in Somerset, as well as in Dorset, in association with a combe seems unlikely. An alternative meaning might be OE **bata** 'a club or a phallus' (pers. comment, John McN. Dodgson). Close to Taunton, the modern Staplegrove takes its name from OE **stapel** + **graf**, 'the wood with the post'. This wood was evidently a holy place, since the field-name 'halgrove', OE **halig** + **graf**, 'the holy grove' still survived in the nineteenth century (D/D/Rt 6). Phallus worship may have been practised here also. Not far from Taunton holy trees still existed as late as the ninth or even the tenth century. To the west of Taunton there was an ash tree described as *þan halgan æsce*, 'the holy ashtree' and again as *quendam fraxinum que imperiti sacrum vocant*, 'a certain ashtree the locals call holy' (BL 15350; S. 311).[2] Such holy trees were probably not uncommon, although other named trees in charters and in place-names are more likely to be references to gallows.

There are three early monastic sites in Somerset, which were in existence by the end of the seventh century: Glastonbury, Muchelney and Frome. At Glastonbury, the excavations have shown the existence of the first stone church built by King Ine (688–726) and dedicated to SS Peter and Paul (Radford 1981, p. 116). This church stood east of a wooden church, which pre-dated it and which was known as the *vetusta ecclesia*, 'the old church'. This building still stood in the twelfth century and was destroyed in the great fire of 24 May 1184. There seems no reason to doubt the tradition that this was the most ancient church on the site (Carley 1978, p. 108). It has also been suggested that an ancient church stood on the site of the present St Benedict's. This building lies directly in line with the ancient and the existing churches and corresponds with the known Anglo-Saxon practice of placing a series of churches one behind another in a row on special sites (Aston and Burrow 1982, pp. 119–20). There may also have existed a vallum, surrounding the monastery

---

[2] The OE quotation appears in the Old English version of the bounds of the charter for Taunton, British Library Add. MSS 15350, ff. 27v–28 and the Latin version in the same manuscript is printed as S. 311 of 854. However, the charter is considered spurious (see Sawyer for details of the authorities). Even if this is so, the OE version certainly has every appearance of being a genuine tenth-century boundary, with the Latin version as a translation.

and enclosing several hectares (Radford 1981, pp. 113–14).

As with so many early monastic establishments, there is no foundation charter for Glastonbury. The first known grant in 678 was for six hides of land on Glastonbury island itself (S. 1666) and this was followed by a stream of grants by private individuals and by rulers. It is important not to exaggerate the extent of the lands of Glastonbury in the seventh and early eighth centuries. Up to the abdication of Ine in 726 the total grants came to about 200 hides (Fig. 4.7). All these grants were reasonably close to the new monastery, which was sited on an island in the marshes, but it was not isolated since it had good communications to the Fosse Way, to the east. Neither should it be assumed that the marshes were granted because they were inhospitable and unprofitable. As we have seen earlier, there were distinct advantages for the community which lived on the edges of marshlands. Many of the estates given to Glastonbury were very similar to Glastonbury itself, in that they were communities on the edge of the Levels. Most of them were to be large and thriving in the Middle Ages.

Muchelney Abbey was founded in a very similar location to Glastonbury, an island in the marshes. The record of the benefactions it received up to 725 is very different from that of Glastonbury, with only forty-six hides recorded in charters.

At Frome a monastery existed by the beginning of the eighth century (Edwards 1986; 1988). St Aldhelm was the founder of this house, which was a daughter of Malmesbury Abbey and he was the head of the community, along with Malmesbury (Hamilton 1870, p. 332). Since this monastery did not prosper and only existed as a secular church by 1086 (DB 1, 8), it provides some clues about the foundation of early monasteries. The eight hides of land which belonged to Frome in 1086 may represent its original endowment, taken out of the multiple estate of the king, whose holding at Frome still amounted to fifty ploughlands of ancient demesne in 1086 (DB 1, 8). Glastonbury and Muchelney may have been endowed in the same way and then have expanded their holdings as a result of their close association with the royal house and with other members of the nobility. However, only Glastonbury in this early period was an outstanding success. There was clearly not room for many monasteries so close to one another, if they hoped to benefit from large gifts of land.

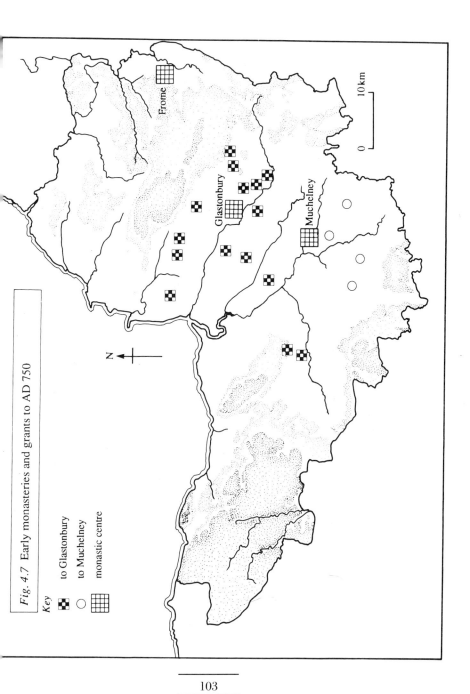

Fig. 4.7 Early monasteries and grants to AD 750

Key
- ▨ to Glastonbury
- ○ to Muchelney
- ▦ monastic centre

Frome

Glastonbury

Muchelney

N

0   10 km

The possibility that Congresbury and Banwell housed monastic communities which were Celtic in origin has been mentioned above. There are no known benefactions to either of these houses and we do not know how large their endowments may have been. They certainly did not flourish under the English rulers of Somerset.

In origin, the monasteries of Somerset do not appear to have been very large institutions, but there were several of them, more than were to be found in other parts of Wessex in the seventh and eighth centuries, with only Malmesbury in Wiltshire and Winchester in Hampshire (Morris 1983, pp. 35–8). This generosity to the church in Somerset at the beginning of the English period can be explained as part of the pattern of appropriation of the countryside. With relatively few retainers to satisfy, both kings and nobility could afford to be generous to the monasteries, especially as they provided English allies in an Old Welsh world in which part of the political battle was fought in ecclesiastical terms, as witness the struggle over the recognition of Roman Easter and the tonsure. Aldhelm, as bishop of Wessex 'West of the Wood', wrote to the Cornish king, Geraint, urging him to observe the Roman Easter (Haddan and Stubbs 1871, 268–73). The dislike of Celtic Christian practice by the strictly orthodox English priesthood may well have been a factor in encouraging action against the Welsh.

Glastonbury was probably sited in such a way as to make visits from Somerton easy, while it was also some distance from Sherborne. Muchelney is also close to several royal estates. None of the early monasteries was sited in the far west of Somerset, which was probably excluded from consideration as a site for foundations because of its remoteness and underdevelopment. Glastonbury certainly became an important centre for religious groups from Ireland. The chapel at Beckery was evidently a focal point for Irish monks in the early eighth century (Rahtz and Hirst 1974), as they passed to and fro, from Ireland to the continent and back. Such contacts must have helped to keep Glastonbury abreast with life in Europe.

The development of the secular church has been seen as separate from that which led to the foundation of the monasteries, but recent work suggests that the division between the two institutions was not at all clear-cut. While the larger minster churches were served by communities of priests, the monasteries also often assumed pastoral responsibility for the lands around the house. The foundation of both monasteries and minsters was primarily the work of the king and they were part of his policy for control of the new lands as well as being devices which helped to knit together his new kingdom (Blair 1988a). A sytem of 'minster' churches, founded at major centres acted as Christian foci for the neighbourhood. A straightforward system such as this would fit well with the idea of the multiple estate, with the king or some other important noble at the centre, directing religous life as well as politics, for the benefit of the West Saxon hegemony. However, there is a great danger in simply assuming that the pattern visible by the mid-eleventh century can be projected backwards into the later seventh and the eighth century. Richard Morris has suggested that most minster churches probably began life on royal estates as chapels for the use of the king and his household (Morris 1989, p. 131). The growth of a 'system' would therefore be quite haphazard, although a genuine pattern would exist.

The are few physical remains of pre-Norman buildings in Somerset and nothing which can be dated to the seventh or the eighth centuries. The evidence must therefore be circumstantial. Place-names show that some churches did exist at an early date, but since the first references to such sites are all late, Ilminster (AD 995), Cheddar mynster (AD 1068), Bedminster (AD 1086), Pitminster (AD 938), Pennard mynster (AD 955), early dates are uncertain. Literary references are similarly difficult. Aldhelm's *Vita* (Hamilton 1870) mentions two churches at Bruton, but these may have been written 'backwards' into the narrative, by the authors or their sources. In the case of Cheddar, King Alfred's will speaks of the community and this is the only firm reference to communities of priests (Keynes and Lapidge 1983). This scepticism is instructive, but ultimately so negative as to be useless. Dr John Blair has offered some criteria for defining minster or collegiate churches, which include references to groups of clergy, endowments of at least one hide of land, separate valuation of their assets in the Domesday Book, tenure of land separately from the main manor, rights over other churches and attachment to royal or episcopal manors (Blair 1985, p. 106). A similar scheme can be applied to Somerset secular churches to test their possible antiquity. The criteria chosen are: archaeological associations other than tenth-century architecture; literary and documentary references; Domesday lands; royal, episcopal, monastic ownership or associations. Each of these criteria are scored from one to five. The higher the score, the greater the probability of an early origin (see Table 4.1). Monasteries have been included in order to avoid artificial divisions.

Table 4.1 Possible church sites prior to AD 750 ranked according to strength of evidence

Site	Archaeology	Documents	DB lands	Owners	Total
Glastonbury	5	5	5	4	19
Wells	5	3	5	5	18
Frome	3	4	5	5	17
Muchelney	3	5	5	4	17
Cheddar	5	5	0	5	15
Ilchester	5	0	4	5	14
Cannington	5	0	3	5	13
Shapwick	2	2	4	4	12
Congresbury	2	3	3	4	12
Carhampton	2	0	4	5	11
Crewkerne	0	0	5	5	10
Bruton	0	4	0	5	9
Ilminster	0	5	0	4	9
S. Petherton	0	0	4	5	9
Milborne	0	0	4	5	9
Taunton	0	3	0	5	8
Brent	0	0	4	4	8
Curry	0	0	3	5	8
N. Petherton	0	0	3	5	8
Chewton	0	0	3	4	7
Williton	0	2	0	5	7
Banwell	0	3	0	3	6
Milverton	0	0	2	4	6
Doulting	0	3	0	2	5
Keynsham	0	0	0	4	4
Stogumber	0	0	4	0	4
Yatton	0	0	4	0	4
Kilmersdon	0	0	3	0	3
Long Ashton	0	0	2	0	2

This table suggests relative age and it does not 'prove' the existence of a church, but merely suggests the likelihood. It is entirely a construct, but it does suggest that the oldest sites are those such as Wells, later the cathedral site, Cheddar, site of a royal palace and Ilchester, close to a Roman town and beside or over a Roman cemetery. Several well-known royal sites are also strongly supported, such as Cannington and Crewkerne. The results have also been expressed on a map (Fig. 4.8). This technique shows the way in which the evidence is strongest in the centre of Somerset, where the royal presence is strongest and where the greatest continuity can be demonstrated. The minster at Northover, just outside Ilchester, probably served as the main church for the royal centre at Somerton, which had no parish church of its own until 1144 (Dunning 1974, p. 147). Here the church was founded beside and probably upon a Roman cemetery, thus sharing in a characteristic of early churches common throughout the western world. Probably a pre-existent Christian site made it unneccessary and perhaps impossible to found a church in Somerton. The existing chapel there was probably for royal use. At Cheddar, the parish church stands beside a Roman villa, another well-documented association for early churches (Morris 1983, p. 43). The association with a very early Christian site at Wells has already been considered and the likelihood is also strong that the church at Cannington represents a successor to a similar early Christian site at the hillfort. At Williton, the parish church of St Decuman is not in the major royal settlement, probably because the association with the Celtic Saint Decuman was too strong for a chapel at the royal hall at Williton to prosper. On the other hand, the churches at Crewkerne, Taunton, Curry and Bruton were probably the chapels of royal vills.

Even at this early date, it seems unlikely that all churches were either royal chapels or minsters. Some small churches also existed. Those which survived from the Old Welsh period included the chapel of St Martin on Marchey, near Wedmore (S. 1253) and the chapel at Leigh, near Street (S. 1249). St Aldhelm's writings suggest that he founded churches in the course of his work (Lapidge and Herren 1979, p. 11) and William of Malmesbury's *Vita* records that he died in a small wooden church on the estate at Doulting (Hamilton 1870, p. 382). There were probably other small chapels and churches, even in the first

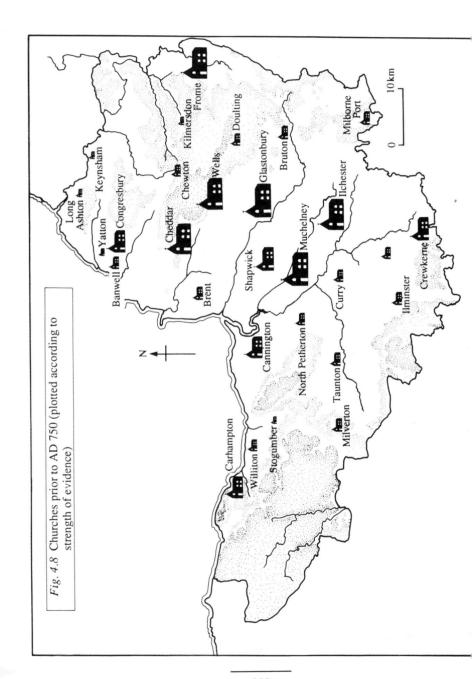

Fig. 4.8 Churches prior to AD 750 (ploted according to strength of evidence)

Long Ashton
Keynsham
Yatton
Congresbury
Banwell
Brent
Cheddar
Chewton
Wells
Kilmersdon
Frome
Doulting
Glastonbury
Bruton
Milborne Port
Shapwick
Muchelney
Ilchester
Cannington
North Petherton
Curry
Ilminster
Crewkerne
Taunton
Carhampton
Williton
Stogumber
Milverton

N

0   10 km

half of the eighth century and they grew in number steadily. By the end of the ninth century, churches were probably quite numerous. Even Aller had a church with baptismal rights when Guthrum was christened there (ASC, AD 878).

The religious community in Somerset did not have its own bishop for the first thirty years after the English conquest. At first, Somerset was simply a part of the West Saxon diocese. On the death of Bishop Haeddi, in 706[3] (Bede, p. 225) the diocese was divided and Aldhelm, the abbot of Malmesbury and founder of Frome, became the first bishop 'West of the Wood'. His cathedral seat was in the abbey at Sherborne, from where he ruled a diocese which covered Somerset, Dorset and those parts of Devon under English rule. The head of the See was to remain at Sherborne until the early tenth century. This site was relatively close to the royal vill at Somerton (and to the Roman road system) as well as being within relatively easy travelling distance of Malmesbury Abbey, with which the saint retained a strong connection. Ecclesiastical authority remained relatively close to the region within which church power and political authority was concentrated, in eastern central Somerset.

Aldhelm's life presents an informative picture of the work of a senior ecclesiastic in the region. He may have been born in Dorset (Porter 1979) and he certainly spent most of his working life in the western parts of Wessex. He was probably related to the royal house, though the traditional suggestion that his father was a brother of King Ine is not soundly based. Traditionally his training is associated with the Celtic monk Maeldubh, but this cannot be supported from any contemporary source. Although some Celtic influence in his education has been detected, his latinity suggests that he had been well trained in a continental tradition (Winterbottom 1977). We know that his later education was at Canterbury under the Roman Hadrian, abbot of the monastery of SS Peter and Paul. By c. 674, Aldhelm was abbot of the new monastery of Malmesbury, founded on the edge of West Saxon territory and, apart from visits to Rome, he spent his life at Malmesbury and in its vicinity. As well as the foundation of daughter monasteries at Bradford-on-Avon and Frome, his

[3] Bede's *Ecclesiastical History of the English Nation* (Everyman Edition, London, 1910), p. 255. The date of Haeddi's death and Aldhelm's accession is corrected in Lapidge and Herren 1979, p. 10.

writings reveal that he rebuilt the monastic church at Malmesbury and also built there two churches dedicated to St Mary and St Michael. His poems of dedication also indicate that he built another church at Malmesbury, dedicated to the Virgin, and that he dedicated an otherwise unknown church to St Matthew. His record was probably similar to that of other leading churchmen of the time, a life of constant activity and travel as the structure of the English church was set in place in close co-operation with the king.

The picture drawn of Somerset in the seventh and eighth centuries is one in which large-scale organisation provides an explanation for the underlying pattern which can still be seen in the landscape: the distribution of major settlements and the relationship of some minor places to them; the existence of a rational pattern of place-names, which makes sense of them; the positioning of important churches and early monastic sites. Although different from the countryside which was to emerge by 1066, the organisation of the shire was far from primitive. It reflected the dominance of the early Wessex kings and their aristocracy. Although they can have formed only a tiny proportion of the nation, they dominated it completely. We do not know how many English peasants moved from Wiltshire with their lords, but clearly there were enough to start to name settlements immediately and eventually to completely rename the landscape, even at the most minor level. The numbers needed for this were probably small. The Welsh, both landowners and peasants, continued to live in the countryside, but institutions such as the church provided a cultural weapon which enabled the English to absorb the Welsh, so that at length their language and all memory of their ancestry was extinguished.

English Somerset was the work of its rulers. Both in the pattern of estates and the growth of the church it was the king who left his mark. He it was gave land to the nascent church or allowed his followers to make grants. He granted estates to his followers or demanded tribute. He laid down the status of the conquered Welsh. The English lived in a landscape already shaped for them by the Welsh, but the shire which had emerged had probably gained its boundaries in essentials as they were to be until recent times. Inside those boundaries great changes were afoot.

1 A view north-westward through the massive stones which form the Stanton Drew stone circles

2 The entrance to Stony Littleton long barrow. The barrow was restored in the nineteenth century, but probably retains much of its original appearance

3   Cadbury Castle, South Cadbury. A view looking northwards with a line of ramparts clearly visible

4   Wansdyke, near Bath. The dyke on the left, looking eastward. The top of the bank is now covered with a dense hedge. The fall to the north now forms the ends of a row of suburban houses

5 The Caractacus Stone, on Winford Hill, Exmoor, is now protected by a shelter. It probably stands where it was erected beside a road, as a memorial. It survived because it became a boundary stone. The inscription is still visible

6 King Æthelred's charter of AD 995 (S. 884) to Muchelney Abbey, confirming land at Ilminster and West Camel (reproduced by permission of Somerset County Council)

8 The tower-turret and south transept of the eleventh-century church of St John at Milborne Port

9 The remains of decorative work on the chancel of Milborne Port church. This fine building is in keeping with the importance of the *burh* and the royal centre which it served

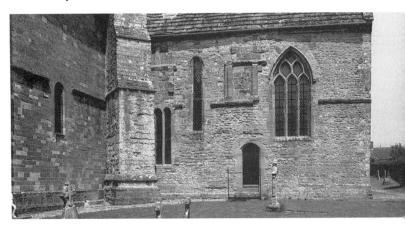

7 Part of the shaft of a cross, probably of the tenth century, now preserved in the church at West Camel. It may have stood in the tenth-century churchyard. This is all that remains of what must have been a magnificent monument, probably destroyed in the post-Saxon period

10 The surviving gatehouse (now a cottage) and walls of the inner bailey of Stogursey Castle

11 This tympanum over the door of the church at Stoke-sub-Hamdon is primitive but recognisably Romanesque

5

War and peace in the countryside

In 809 Harun al-Rashid, the great Caliph of Baghdad, died and a civil war began to determine the succession. His death marked the point at which a sharp decline in the wealth and influence of the Abbasid caliphate began and with political instability came a sharp decline in the trade of the moslem world, a decline which had its influence upon the economy of the north-west of Europe (Hodges and Whitehouse 1983). There is good reason to see the attacks of the Danes, which first became a real problem in England in 835 when the first serious raids began in the east, as linked to the decline in trade (Stenton 1947, p. 239). On the continent, the problem was exacerbated by the break up of the Carolingian Empire, itself in part precipitated by Harun's death. There, those who sought to exploit the growing weakness of central authority were prepared to ally themselves with the raiders, thus increasing their power and helping to make warfare and raiding a viable alternative way of life (McKitterick 1983, pp. 230–5). They also introduced the idea that raids might be bought off with cash, so that between booty and tribute the wealth flowing back to Denmark gave enormous political power to those who led the raids, making them an institution in Danish society.

The Danish raiders launched themselves upon a Wessex where it is likely that the polity was already under some strain. The collapse of trade with the continent – caused by the dislocation of contacts with northern Francia as civil war intensified from the 820s – has been suggested as the reason for this outburst of aggression by the West Saxons. Under King Egbert, in 825, the men of Wessex defeated the Mercians and then proceeded to conquer Kent and receive the submission of Essex and Surrey (Stenton 1947, pp. 229–30). Although the domination of Mercia did not last long, the south-east of England remained under Wessex control, often used as an appanage for the king's eldest son. The effect of Egbert's success against the Mercians was that the Midlands and East Anglia became much weaker politically, so that, as in Francia, the Danes were able to take advantage of the situation to raid and to extract tribute. Once resistance in the Midlands and the north of England was overcome the Danes were free to turn their attention to the south and in turn to put pressure upon Wessex, and it was that military pressure which was to trigger the major developments in West Saxon society during the tenth century.

It is apparent that by the middle of the ninth century, if not before, there existed a mechanism for the use of the military power of individual shires. King Æthelwulf lost a battle with thirty-five shiploads of Danes at Carhampton in 843 but in 848 the men of Somerset and the men of Dorset, led by ealdorman Eanwulf of Somerset, ealdorman Osric of Dorset and the bishop Ealhstan of Sherborne defeated another raiding party at the mouth of the Parrett, and there are, of course, many other references to the shire levies (ASC). But the army commanded either by the king or by the ealdorman of the shire was almost certainly not very large. It was composed of the warriors of the shire, supported by retainers from their estates (Abels 1988, pp. 58–60), probably drawn from the class of ceorls, the free peasantry. In addition, when the king led an army he was also surrounded by the members of his household, who formed his personal warband. It was this system which the sons of Æthelwulf used against the Danes.

When we consider the size and wealth of the kingdom of Wessex and then consider how near Alfred came to defeat at the hands of the Danes it becomes clear that the system which relied upon the loyalty to the king of his chief followers was barely adequate to meet the challenge. By 878 Alfred was reduced to hiding in the marshes at Athelney supported only by his household retainers and Æthelnoth the ealdorman of Somerset – according to Æthelweard (Campbell 1962, p. 42). At this site they built a fort, probably an earthen construction consisting of a ditch and bank with a palisade fence, which was still recognisable in the mid-tenth century when the charter for Lyng was written, where it was *the old herworth*, 'the old army enclosure' (S. 432).

Alfred's courage and tenacity (as well as the reduction in the size of the Viking armies as more and more men left to settle in Mercia) go some way to explain why he was able to force Guthrum and his followers to accept Christianity and withdraw from Wessex in 878 (ASC). When the next great military challenge from the Danes came between 893 and 896 Alfred proved himself more than a match for them. Despite their attacks the heartland of Wessex was not touched, giving the king the economic base from which to resist (Wormald 1982, pp. 149–50). The king's careful rebuilding of his military capacity and the development of the *burhs* as fortifications against the Vikings ensured the long-term survivial of the West Saxon dynasty.

Property and obligation

By the beginning of the ninth century it is likely that the great royal and princely multiple estates were under attack, broken up by the kings of Wessex as the result of social and political pressures from their aristocratic followers. A good deal of evidence for this process and the granting of bookland instead, can be found in the 'Decimation of Æethelwulf' (Abels 1988, p. 61), but other evidence is also to be found in other charters. An estate at Ditcheat was granted to Eanwulf the *princeps* of King Æthelwulf in 842, the man who, in 848, was the ealdorman of Wessex who won the battle against the Danes at the mouth of the Parrett (ASC). This large estate of thirty hides later passed to Glastonbury Abbey and had probably been a part of the royal multiple estate at Bruton. It is possible that Ditcheat was a reward for his loyalty. By the latter part of the ninth century, the granting of land as 'bookland' was far advanced in Wessex. Under the older system of landholding, on the multiple estates, men owed their service to the king, or some other prince, as a result of their positions as his tenants. Once land was granted away by 'book' it became, in some sense, the hereditary property of the grantee and at first had no military obligation, since bookland was a method of tenure initially used to endow the church. By the mid-ninth century, the kings of Wessex were enforcing a duty of military service upon their aristocracy who lived on bookland, but they also drew service from the retainers on their own estates. When Alfred was at bay in Somerset, he lurked there partly because the Somerset marshes were so inaccessible in winter, but also because some of his largest estates were in the shire, from which he might expect support and soldiers. Even with military service enforced upon bookland the supply of soldiers was clearly not enough and there is evidence that Alfred alienated church property in an attempt to provide more land for retainers and thus ensure their loyalty. Creech St Michael may have been granted to a thegn by King Alfred for this reason, as may Puriton (Fleming 1985). Many other estates which had originally belonged to the church were in secular hands by the tenth century, and while some of these estates may have been seized by laymen in difficult times or granted away on leases and never resumed, many were probably the result of seizure by the king, who added them to his own estates or granted them away to a follower as 'bookland'. In this way in 973 King Edgar granted Berrow to a thegn, Wulmer (S. 793). Originally Berrow had lain inside the estate of Brent and so must have become detached and come into the king's hand. The grant to a thegn suggests that it was being used by the king to endow his warriors, but by 1066 it was back in the hands of Glastonbury, perhaps given by the thegn or by his family, which is why we know something of its tenth-century history. Probably many other estates passed through a similar process.

Alfred's successors continued his policies by ensuring that the West Saxon state was able to raise the soldiers it needed for its defence. During the early tenth century it became the normal practice that all bookland was held on condition that military service should be performed for it (Abels 1988, see chapter 6). In addition, the king demanded service from all the great land-owners. As a result, the tenth century saw two great developments: one was the growth of the military class as the king's demand for soldiers increased; the other was the growth in population stimulated by relative peace and by the extended exploitation of the countryside.

There is no doubt that, by the beginning of the tenth century, the multiple estate had largely ceased to exist. The countryside, outside the core of large royal estates and some of the surviving church estates, now consisted of a large number of individual units, some of which survived through the whole Anglo-Saxon period, chiefly because they were granted to the church during the tenth century. For example, the estate of Pilton, as granted to Glastonbury Abbey in AD 705 (S. 248), has a set of bounds of the tenth century which cover an area including the later parishes of Pilton, Croscombe and part of Shepton Mallet. These bounds are typical for a large estate of this type, running, in large part, along streams and major Roman roads. Generally, the bounds are simple and direct. At Ditcheat, another large estate which probably came into the hands of Glastonbury Abbey in the mid-tenth century, the bounds again follow the Fosse Way, then another unrecognised Roman road, as well as several streams (S. 292). Many of these larger ecclesiastical estates survived into the eleventh century and beyond, as did many large royal estates. Of the thirty-six estates in the Domesday Book which were of fifteen hides and greater, only four were not owned by the crown or by churches and monasteries in 1066. Of the seventy-six estates of ten hides and above, only twenty-eight belonged to men who were outside the circle of church and court (DB).

Some of the earliest portions detached from the great multiple estates may survive as units carrying names of the type 'personal name + ingtun'. Settlements with names of this type in Somerset tend to be grouped together. Particularly prominent are two groups, one around Frome, a royal centre, the other close to Ilminster (Fig. 5.1). Although there is considerable variation in the sizes of these estates, they average just over six hides, while the run of ordinary non-royal and non-church estates average only 3.12 hides. Part of the reason for this is that the 'ington' type estates are in the east of the county, where the bulk of the royal and church estates are to be found, while the average size of estates is deeply affected by the large number of very small units in the far west of the county, but in addition these estates do not seem to have suffered the division characteristic of other places. It seems that, when new estates were hived off at an early date, comparatively large grants of land were made. The recipients

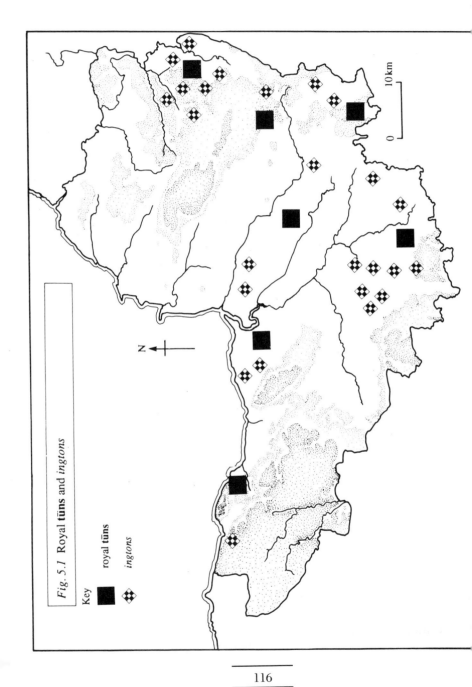

Fig. 5.1 Royal **tūns** and *ingtons*

Key

■ royal **tūns**

◈ *ingtons*

N

10 km

0

were probably not important men and were not greatly affected by later social developments.

However, the mass of estates in existence in the tenth and eleventh centuries were very small. Of the 891 estates in the Domesday Book which existed in 1066, 485 were of three hides or less and no less than 273 estates were of less than one hide. An obvious question, therefore, is how this pattern emerged. This question is especially important when it is realised that many estates were surprisingly stable over long periods. This is true even for places which were not in the hands of the king or the church. It seems certain that a uniform system for the assessment of estates for military service had been built upon the older system which regulated the payment of tribute. The hide provided a way of rating all estates. Every time that an estate is mentioned in a charter of the tenth century its hidage is given, and in many cases, the hidage of the mid-tenth century is preserved in the Domesday record. Of 71 charters, some known only from summaries or indexes, which carry a hidage, 37 agree with the Domesday Book figure. A great many of the estates with un-changing assessment became church property, which explains why their charters survived, but where this did not happen it is possible to see that land often changed hands. At West Camel, near Yeovil, the estate, probably of six hides, was first granted in 939 × 46 by King Edmund to the thegn Ælfgar (S. 1718); again in 955 × 9 by King Eadwig to the thegn Cinric (S. 1755); in 959 × 75 by King Edgar to the thegn Brihtric and finally in 995 we find that Abbot Leofric of Muchelney Abbey had purchased the estate, added to it four hides given by the ealdorman Æthelmere (probably Downhead) and added it to the Abbey's lands, where it was to remain (DB 9, 7). In much the same way, King Edmund granted Corston, near Bath, to his minister Aethelnoth in 941 (S. 476); King Eadwig granted it to the lady Ælfswith in 956 (S. 593); and it was finally granted by King Edgar to Bath Abbey in 972 (S. 785). Throughout these transactions it retained the same hidage, along with its fixed boundaries.

Other land undoubtedly changed hands for money. Monasteries often bought land in the tenth century. Bath Abbey paid King Edgar 100 *mancuses* of gold in part exchange for the estate of Clifton, near Bath (S. 777). Laymen also bought and sold land. Britric Grim revealed in his will that he had and added an extra hide of land to his estate at Rimpton by purchase (Whitelock 1930). This market in land must have stimulated the break-up of land units, as did the Old English habit of division of property among heirs. Where a landowner was wealthy this would mean the dispersal of estates, but where the person in question owned only a single estate it would be split. By the time the Domesday Book was made this process had gone some way to break up estates. This might explain why Vexford was split into two estates, each with the same name and each of half a hide in 1066 (DB 21, 44; 45). It is noticeable that when estates were divided in this way, lordship was divided at the same time. It seems likely that the landmarket chiefly affected the class who expected to have lordship over other men.

However, the largest influence upon the size of estates and the major reason for the multiplication of small or medium-sized estates lay in the division of lands by lords during the tenth century, primarily to reward their own followers and to provide for the military service now demanded of them by the kings of the English. This was a practice followed by all landowners, although it is most obvious upon church estates. The best example of this is at Shapwick. This estate first came into the hands of Glastonbury Abbey in 729 (S. 253). The bounds of the charter describe a very large estate which covered the Polden Hills from just west of Street and probably stretched westward as far as Woolavington, including areas of marshland on both the northern and southern sides. Shapwick, after which the estate was later named, included within it much of the Sweet track, and field name evidence[1] (Egerton 3321 and Costen 1989) and recent field archaeology suggests that the estate had an agricultural history during the Roman period and it is possible that a substantial Roman building awaits discovery. In 1983 Nicholas Corcos suggested that Shapwick and its surrounding villages, Ashwick, Sutton, Edington, Chilton and Catcott were part of a planned landscape, with regularly divided estates, planned fields and

---

[1] 'Abchester'. This name appears in numerous sources for the estate, starting with the British Library, Egerton MS. 3321 of 1327. See M. Costen, 'A survey of the Manor of Shapwick in 1327 from the Egerton Manuscript 3321 in the British Library', in M. A. Aston (ed.), *The Shapwick Project; a Topographical and Historical Survey, 2nd report* (Bristol 1989), pp. 79–86.

planned village layouts. He suggested that they were all planned and laid out at the same time (Corcos 1984). This was clearly not a very early event. The parish church of Shapwick is also the ancient parish church of Edington, Moorlinch, Sutton Mallet, Chilton Polden, Catcott and Stawell, suggesting that it had been founded before the estate broke up into its constituent units. Since the abbey of Glastonbury was in decline during the first forty years of the tenth century, it is unlikely that the division took place before the abbacy of Dunstan, which began c. 946. However, this division had occurred before 1066, since the constituent units were named as existing separately in the Domesday Survey (DB 8, 5 and Holmes 1896, I, pp. 27, 73) (Fig. 5.2). If the division and the planning of these new villages had occurred at a very early date, that is to say at the time of the first English settlements in the later seventh century, or in the early eighth century, we might have expected to see the church integrated in the village, but it was not. Instead it stood in the fields, 500 metres from the village centre and in 1331 it was finally abandoned in favour of the present parish church in Shapwick, which had been built because of the inconvenient location of the old church (Costen 1991b). It seems certain that the villages were built long after the church. The church represents an element in a landscape which was superseded by the division of the estate, the laying out of open-fields and the building of new villages where none had previously existed.

Numerous other examples of estates which were split in this way have come to light. This is likely to be the explanation for the existence of many of the villages in Somerset which carry names of the 'East and West', 'North and South' variety. Good examples include, East, Middle and West Chinnock, North and South Barrow and East and West Lydford (Costen 1991b). The deserted medieval hamlet at Eckweek south of Bath is probably another example. Recent excavation work suggests that it first came into existence as a small settlement in the tenth century (Kidd 1989). As in some other cases there is evidence that suggests that the settlement was planned. It is difficult otherwise to explain how it came to possess a detached portion of meadow, just as East Lydford held a detached portion of woodland and West Chinnock had a detached East Field.

It is probable that many of the settlements with names of

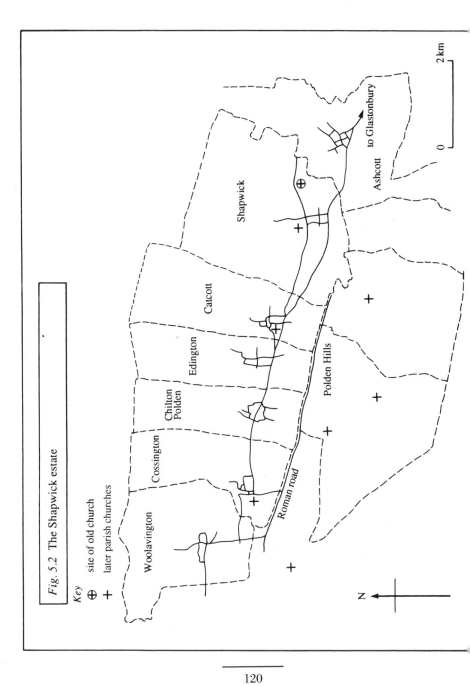

Fig. 5.2 The Shapwick estate

Key
⊕ site of old church
+ later parish churches

a simple type, 'personal name + tun' appeared at this time. Examples would be the Allertons, near Wedmore (Ælfweard's tun), Durston (Deor's tun), Lufton (Lufa's tun) and Shearston (Sigered's tun) (Ekwall 1960). They represent estates made from new, complete with new villages, founded in order to supply a dependent thegn with a benefice which would support him, in return for his service to his lord, the owner of the land.

Many of these dependent thegns were listed as the holders of these small estates in the Domesday Survey. These men were such minor figures that the survey often fails to give their names, just recording them as 'thegns'. At Woolston, near South Cadbury, the estate of three hides one and a half virgates was held by three thegns in 1066 (DB 19, 55). Cloford, an estate of ten hides, was held by five thegns (DB 19, 53). At Shapwick, although the church of Glastonbury itself farmed Shapwick, the dependent estates were held by a group of fourteen thegns in 1066 (DB 8, 5). The subject status of many of these thegns is revealed on many church estates, where it is frequently stated that 'he could not be separated from the church'. Some parts of Domesday estates, again church land, are stated to be *thegnland*, suggesting its use as benefices to support military retainers (DB 5, 20). The great monasteries of the tenth and eleventh centuries, after their refoundation in the mid-century, became very important landowners. By 1066 Glastonbury had 181 hides of land granted to eighty tenants, all of dependent status. Unfortunately, the Domesday Survey in Somerset does not note the status of most of the thegns on estates which were not in church hands. Where they are not shown as able to 'go where they would with their land' it is likely that they too were in positions of dependence upon some secular overlord. They formed a class several hundred strong and probably occupied about a quarter of the land in the county.

Of course, where lords owned their own land, there was nothing to stop them subdividing an estate when the property passed by inheritance. Partible inheritance among sons was a normal practice and must have affected estates to some degree. However, as open-field agriculture emerged in the tenth century, the spread of the open fields must have discouraged the physical subdivision of estates.

A complicated pattern of estates had emerged by the later

tenth century. Some had survived almost untouched from previous centuries, but such were rare. Most multiple estates had broken up into smaller units. A small minority of these units were large, but most were small. Many of the smaller estates which were visible in 1066 and still exist today as parishes were simply parts of larger estates, individual farmsteads or hamlets, used as the basis for independent units. As individual farm units, they had existed for centuries. In the tenth century they were used as the nucleus around which was founded a village with its fields. In this way, places such as Badgeworth or Closworth became villages. Others were carved out of larger estates and developed new names formed with a personal name and **tun**, such as Allerton or Lufton. Many others were formed by the division of unitary estates, giving rise to similarly named estates lying next to one another – the 'North Barrow, South Barrow' type.

The formation of estates in this period was probably definitive. The bounds which emerged in the tenth century were the bounds of estates, which were later to be described in the Domesday Survey for Somerset as manors and which often appear as parishes from the later twelfth century onwards. In tenth century charters where there is a bound described it can often still be traced, and although deviations from the later parish boundary do occur they are rarely significant. I have shown that the estate at Rimpton has boundaries which diverge from those of the later parish at only one point as the result of the purchase of land in the mid-tenth century (Costen 1985). At Ditcheat the boundary laid down in the charter of 842 (S. 292) was probably not described until the abbey of Glastonbury obtained the property, perhaps not till the mid-tenth century, but was probably already defined by 842 (Costen 1988, pp. 46–7). It is probable that the boundary of Hornblotton was defined by 855 x 860 when it was granted to the same layman who held Ditcheat (S. 1699, a lost charter by King Æthelbald to Eanulf). In the north of Somerset, the bounds of the Domesday estates at Stanton Prior, Corston and Priston were laid down in the charters of the mid-tenth century and can still be identified (Costen 1983). The same is certainly true of many other estates in the Bath area: at Bathford, South Stoke and Clifton and at North Stoke as well. Although this last has a charter of the mid-eighth century, it is likely that the boundaries are tenth century (S. 265). There seems little doubt that the pattern of lordship and the patchwork of estates visible in the Domesday Book was established during this period.

This pattern of development predominated in the lower-lying, more fertile eastern part of the shire but to the west a different course was followed. On the large and lowlying estates the eastern pattern was also present. Williton itself was a royal estate of the lowland type but in the Carhampton hundred, thirty-six settlements were enumerated in the Domesday Book, although only Carhampton itself was of any size, perhaps twenty hides. The other thirty-five estates averaged only 0·94 hides each and many were only virgates. It seems that these represented very small land units, too small in many cases to be more than a single farm or a hamlet, which had started as settlements amidst the waste of the slopes of Exmoor and the Brendon Hills. These units could not be subdivided into estates which would support dependent thegns. However, there is evidence that here, too, considerable change occurred during the tenth century.

In the Domesday Book the hidage of each estate was used as a method of assessment for taxation purposes. Recent work by McDonald and Snooks has shown that there is a relationship between the hidage of Domesday estates and their money values which is constant enough to be statistically significant in the counties examined (McDonald and Snooks 1986). However, Nicholas Higham has recently shown that the 'ploughland' of the Domesday Book is a record of the actual amount of ploughland in use each of the manors surveyed (Higham 1991b). It is, therefore, a real measure of the economic activity of each community where it is recorded. As we have seen above, there is good reason to think that once the rating of an estate in hides was fixed, early in the tenth century, there were few occasions to change it, except on division of an estate, when the new units bore their proportion of the burden of the whole of the former estate, or when a preferential down-rating was granted to a friend or relative by the king, as for instance at Puriton, which belonged to Queen Edith in 1066 (DB 11, 1) or at Crowcombe (DB 19, 7) which belonged to St Swithun's at Winchester and paid only for four hides although it was rated at ten. Such exemptions were rare in Somerset. This meant that there was little allowance made for changes in capacity or output from an estate. If estates kept the same relative ranking, one to another, then if an estate expanded cultivation and thus output, this increase would not be subject to extra taxation unless the whole county were subject to an across the board increase in the 'poundage' of the tax. The idea that the hidage and the ploughlands represent two different ways of assessing the capacity of the estate, the first of ancient origin, the second new, appears to conflict with the relationship between hides and cash values. However, it cannot be denied that the effect is real in Somerset and in Devon also. A good example which illustrates the force of the two different ways of looking at estates is provided by Huish in Nettlecombe (DB 31, 3). There were two **hiwisces** in Nettlecombe, now represented by Beggearn Huish and Lodhuish. One of the two settlements was rated for the geld at one and a half hides. However, it contained six ploughlands. The geld rating surely reflects the small size of the estate at the time when the geld was first assessed. The ploughlands represented the real extent of cultivation by 1086. It is inconceivable that this can represent anything but a change in real capacity over a period of time. Although soil quality varies it is difficult to imagine that Huish had always had six ploughlands in use to provide its one and a half hides of taxable capacity.

As compared with the thirty-three hides of the hundred of Carhampton, the number of ploughlands was just over 140. If this represented a real change in capacity or output over the course of the period c. 900 to 1086, then the Carhampton area had seen an expansion of 327 per cent. The same scale of increase is apparent in the whole of west Somerset, suggesting that there had been a dramatic expansion of agriculture, and by implication of population, in the district. In fact west Somerset shares many characteristics with Devon, where similar wide disparities between the hidage and the available ploughlands are apparent.

When examined across the whole county the contrast between the highland and lowland areas of Somerset is quite striking. The most representative value for the increase as between hidage and ploughlands is up to 100 per cent, with the mean at 61 per cent. This type of increase is scattered randomly across the county. It is the norm and just over 29 per cent of estates fall into this category. In 19 per cent of cases the hidage and the ploughlands are the same but in only 9 per cent do they show a negative figure. Some 25 per cent of all estates show an increase greater than 100 per cent and they are overwhelmingly concentrated in the area to the west of the river Parrett. Conversely, the region where there is least disparity between the hidage and the plough-lands is in the east of the county. South of the Mendips only 20 per cent of the land area of the county lies to the east of the Fosse way and yet 50 per cent of all unchanged holdings are there.

The implication of all this is that the tenth century saw a dramatic expansion in the economy of the county as a whole, but that the biggest expansion was in the relatively underdeveloped west. In the south-east, the old heartland of the county, growth, although not absent, was relatively less impressive. Some estates even slipped back.

The only way in which the economy could expand was through the growth of cultivation. We know very little about the early methods of farming in the county, although the subject has been much discussed at a national level (Rowley 1981). It is no longer considered axiomatic that the open-field system was part of the cultural baggage of the first English settlers. In Somerset there is no evidence to suggest that the open-field system was in use before the ninth century and we do not know for certain how arable cultivation was organised, though there is a good deal of speculation pointing to individual farmsteads. The **hiwisc** may well have been a unit of this kind, although we know nothing of its internal agricultural organisation. Did it have fields of the type we are used to today, that is to say 'closes', or did it have a minature two-field system, with the major difference that only one cultivator worked the whole system? Perhaps the German system of blocks of cultivation behind each croft, used in severalty as arable, but open to common grazing was employed. Was the early **wyrth** an individual farmstead, as the Laws of Ine certainly suggest (Fox 1981, pp. 86–7)? For Somerset the evidence is still not available.

In the tenth century such written information as there is about agriculture, is to be found in the charters. The boundary clauses are designed to provide unambigous information about the course of the bound and in doing so they often describe the countryside in considerable detail. Most of the terms used in the sixty-four surviving sets of bounds relate to features such as ditches, trees, hedges and streams, but a minority are terms which describe land-use. **Feld**, a word which probably still meant 'a stretch of open ground' occurs nine times in charters. At Corston, near Bath, there was a reference to *ofer feld on þa riht land gemære*, 'over the field along the straight boundary' (S. 593 of 956). In the post-Conquest period there is evidence that this boundary did indeed run between two areas of open-field, in Corston and in Stanton Prior, and it is the only good candidate in the county for open-field. Elsewhere, as for instance at Pitminster, it is clear that **feld** was rough grazing ground. It was called **oxenafeld**, 'the oxens' field', and it lay on a steep hillside (S. 1006 of 1044). Not far away, at Lydeard there was an area called **fasingafeld**, 'the field of Fasa's men' (S. 380 of 899 × 909). The form of the name, with its **inga** element shows that this was an early English name. As with the previous example it was on a hillside and sounds, from its name, to have been a grazing ground. Both examples probably reflect the rather broken and wooded state of the countryside in this part of Somerset in the seventh and early eighth centuries. Other examples from the east of the county, for example at Batcombe (S. 462 of 940), also seem to show a contrast with ground which is wooded.

Other words indicative of arable cultivation are **æcer** and **furlang**. Several examples of **æcer** appear around Bath, at Weston, Clifton and Marksbury (S. 508 of 946, S. 777 of 970 and S. 431 of 936), but all seem to refer to isolated plots of land rather than fields and the same is true for examples at Wrington and High Ham. Only one reference to **furlang** occurs, at Marksbury, but here the bounds of the charter were probably modified in the twelfth century, so that the word may well refer to the post-Conquest landscape (Costen 1983).

If the written evidence for the existence of open-field is sparse, the evidence from field archaeology is a little stronger. The estate at Chinnock has already been mentioned. It seems likely that this place had started the tenth century as a single unit and was probably still one unit when it was described in the will of Wynflæd *c.* 950 (Whitelock 1930, pp. 10–15, no. iii). By 1066 it was three units, East, West and Middle Chinnock. Originally it had been a fourteen-hide estate and it had been split into three unequal parts. East Chinnock remained the most important, a seven-hide unit, held in 1066 by Edmer Ator, a major Somerset landholder. Middle and West Chinnock had become three-hide and four-hide estates respectively, both of which show clear signs of planning in their fields. In both cases the open-fields were laid out parallel to the boundaries. The boundary between West and Middle Chinnock is a straight line and had clearly been drawn before the fields were laid out. There is every indication that these fields were all planned at the same time. It seems very unlikely that this would have taken place at any other time than when the estate was divided. Furthermore, West Chinnock has its east field on the eastern side of Middle Chinnock, so that it was necessary to go through Middle Chinnock to get to the east field if you were a West Chinnock farmer (Fig. 5.3). No clearer instance could be imagined for evidence that the fields were laid out and that they were laid out at the command of some person in authority. It is impossible to imagine that a group of peasants could have arrived at so inconvenient a solution to an agricultural problem by agreement among themselves.

The newly discovered tenth-century settlement at Eckweek had an open-field system based upon two fields. Here it was the meadow which was detached, and lay down by the river in Shoscombe, at Oxenham. Meadow was a part of the open-field system, and once again was probably laid out along with the fields, when the settlement was planned. At North and South Barrow a unitary estate was divided before the Norman Conquest and two villages founded, each with its own open-field system, with the two sets of fields abutting one another. Again it seems unlikely that they would have grown up spontaneously in this way unless the villages were first planted deliberately. At Shapwick, where a group of settlements were laid out along the Polden Hills, the open-fields are clearly connected with the newly laid out boundaries and with the village site (Costen 1991b). The same relationship between boundaries and new estates and the fields is to be seen at East and West Lydford, and may well appear at other settlements, as yet uninvestigated. Unfortunately we do not yet have enough topographical evidence of open-fields across the county to say much more about their origins. David N. Hall, writing about the Midlands, has argued for a process of planning which would have involved the laying out of very large systems across extensive areas of land – systems which were later 'individualized' by the process of subdivision and exchange (Hall 1985). This was a ninth/tenth-century development. In Somerset

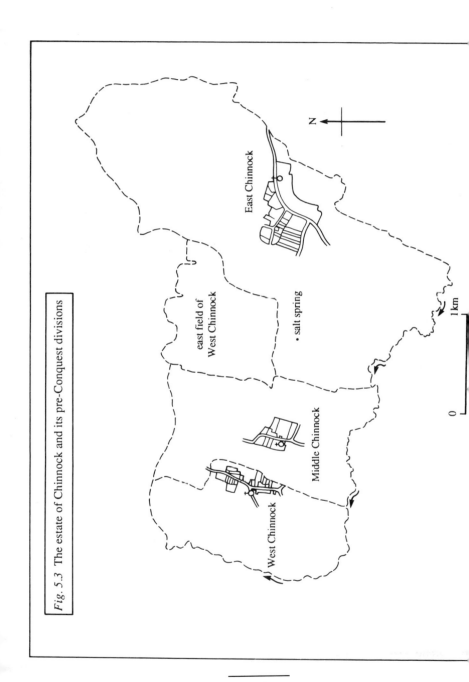

Fig. 5.3 The estate of Chinnock and its pre-Conquest divisions

the growth of the system seems to have taken place at a slightly later date, and it seems doubtful if it could have been very systematic.

Even if open-field agriculture was well established in 'new' settlements in the tenth century, we do not know when it was introduced into the older estates, those owned by the church and by the king. The impulse towards the adoption of the open-field system came from the needs of the ruling class and their new military dependents. Two broad reasons for the growth of the open-field can be suggested. The first of these is that as the old pattern of multiple estates broke up the new smaller units needed to be as self-sufficient as possible. That meant that, everywhere, some grain had to be grown. In addition, given that there were too many of the new military class to be supported mainly from tribute and renders, it was necessary that they should expand their own farming activities. Open-field farming provided them with a large enough peasant clientage to work the lord's land, without substantial investment. The lord's home farm, the demesne, was the vehicle by which the surplus of the peasantry could be diverted to the lord's use, through labour service. The advantage that this system gave to lords who exploited it would have been enough to encourage its extension, where topography made it possible. Since there were more 'lords' in the countryside than there had ever been before, there was a need for more demesne farmland than ever before; open-field made it easier to exploit the demesne. The dispersal of individual holdings through the open-fields was simply a strategy to make sure that each of the small-holdings allocated to the tenants received roughly equal quality of soil. Fairness would have been at once a principle and also a way of making calculation of standard labour services and rents easy to achieve. The lord's land, in contrast, was often grouped into large blocks in each field, suggesting that the lord's land was chosen and laid out first, probably on the best ground.

Villages – the grouping together of all the peasant cultivators' houses and their appurtenant buildings into one settlement which serves the whole estate – are simply a consequence of the existence of open-field agriculture. David Hall has suggested as much for the Midlands (Hall 1985). As we have seen, some villages exhibit a plan, suggesting that they were laid out along with the fields around them for the new villagers. We would expect that the villages would have been grouped near the lord's hall, the post-Norman 'manor house', but no rural example has ever been excavated in Somerset. The site at Cheddar, a king's house, was much larger than the ordinary rural lord's house and the newly discovered site at Milborne Port is an urban example. In places which were not 'new villages', where an established community adopted the new system of agriculture the growth of the village followed naturally, although it may not have happened very quickly. We do not know how long individual farmsteads may have stayed outside the open-field system. At Crewkerne the settlement of Hewish was initially part of the royal estate and was still recognisable as a separate settlement in the early thirteenth century (Dunning 1978, pp. 83–4). In those areas not physically suited to the new methods, the old hamlets persisted, so that **hiwisces** and **wyrths** frequently survive as farmsteads or small groups of farmsteads in the west of the county, while they have disappeared elsewhere. Sweetworthy, a deserted medieval farmstead near Dunkery Beacon is one of many examples (Aston 1985, pp. 83–4). Many others also survive and there is good reason to believe that the pattern of existing and deserted farmstead sites which can still be seen on the higher ground of the western part of the county is based upon an even older pattern than that of the Middle Ages and that its origins should be sought in the Roman and Celtic landscape (Aston 1989b).

There were other consequences for the landscape of Somerset which followed from the expansion of arable agriculture. We have already seen that Somerset was a county which had been well wooded at an early period. The tenth-century charter bounds have frequent references to woodland which are often found on the edge of estates. The impression given is that these were woods which were fenced or surrounded by hedge and bank, preserved carefully as a resource. At Weston, near Bath, there are references to three separate woods, one called *kynges wudu*, and to a **hlipgete**, 'a leapgate' (S. 508), which was a device which allowed animals, particularly deer, to leave the wood but not to enter it. This would only have been necessary if the wood had a fence or a bank and ditch with a fence around it. Once each settlement needed its own wood supply for everyday use the pressure to preserve the woodlands would have become very strong and the shrinking asset would need to be conserved with banks or fences. Estates with 'wood names', such as Adber (**eatan beares**, 'Eata's wood' in 956) or Timsbury (*Timesberie*, 'timber wood' in 1086) are actually quite rare, suggesting that few settlements were carved out of woodland at a late date.

There was little to suggest that the growth of settlement and the expansion of farming was of any great advantage to peasant families who worked the land. Ælfric, who wrote his *Colloquium* as an exercise for tenth-century schoolboys, was describing the world they knew when he made his ploughman say 'O Lord, I work hard. I go out at daybreak and lead the oxen to the fields and yoke them to the plough. No matter how bitter the winter I dare not loiter at home for fear of my lord, but I yoke the oxen and fix the share and turn the land with the plough. Every day I must plough a full acre or more . . . it is a great labour, for I am not free' (Thorpe 1868, p. 19). Domesday bears out the ploughman's statement, for about 16 per cent of the recorded population were slaves (Darby 1977, pp. 342–5). Slightly more light is thrown on the circumstances of the peasantry in the mid-tenth century by Wynflæd's will (Whitelock 1930, pp. 10–15). When disposing of the estate at Chinnock she stated 'And Gerburg is to be freed, and Miscin and Hi . . . and the daughter of Burhulf at Chinnock, and Ælfsige and his elder daughter, and Ceolstan's wife.' When she came to dispose of property she said 'And with regard to the estate at Chinnock, the community at Shaftesbury possess it after her death, and she owns the stock and the men; this being so, she grants to the community the peasants who dwell on the rented land, and the bondmen she grants to her son's daughter Eadgifu . . . And of the bondmen at Chinnock she bequeathes to Eadwold, Ceolstan, Eadstan's son, and Ælffa's son, and Burhwyn [and] Martin and Hisfig'. The ease with which people could be transferred between 'owners' suggests how simple it would have been to transfer families to a new estate. The increase in population was probably not Malthusian. Rather, it is likely that the formation of new settlements and the internal replanning of existing estates made it possible for new farmsteads to be created and encouraged the formation of new peasant households.

We know so little about the status of the peasantry in Old English society that it is difficult to say much about the changes in their conditions, but it is obvious from information in wills, as well as in manumissions and other documents, that the slaves in Old English society were chattels and that a hierarchy of freedom existed among rural dwellers in the tenth and the eleventh centuries. As we have seen from the wills quoted above, dependence was a fact of life and it seems likely that the new structure of estates was a concomitant of a depression in status and a loss of freedom among the peasants. Grouping the peasants together in order to exploit their surpluses more efficiently brought them into closer dependence upon the lord of the community. The imposition of labour services as a way of cultivating the demesne, although based upon the existence of personal service as an expression of man-master relationships, served to strengthen the servile tie and depress status.

For the peasant of the tenth century, the best living was probably to be had upon a church or royal estate. The second half of the tenth century saw the rebirth of English monasticism, led by St Dunstan and his refoundation of Glastonbury. A consequence of that revival was the resumption of lands by the refounded monasteries and the transfer of very large tracts of land to the monasteries, from both kings and noblemen. By 1066, Glastonbury Abbey owned 416 hides in Somerset. Through the Domesday Book, it is possible to establish the value of the estates and compare one estate with another. On Glastonbury estates the return per ploughland averaged 58·76 pence. On secular estates the return was 62·63 pence. Lay landlords squeezed more from their estates than did the church. This was probably something to do with the size of the estate, since there was a negative correlation between the size of church estates and their return to the Abbey. The larger the estate, the worse the return per ploughland. The same was true for the king's estates, although the difference between the king's estates and other secular estates was not so great and the king's absolute return was much better, 78·93 pence per ploughland. It seems likely that, although the Abbey had exploited its lands in the new way, it did not need to press its tenants as hard as the smaller lay landlord. This was probably because the church had been able to rely for nearly a century on gifts of land from the laity. When the monastery needed more funds it persuaded someone to make a donation, rather than setting out to be an efficient estate manager (Costen 1991a, forthcoming).

What has been outlined above is an argument for the development of a new pattern of settlement in the county in the tenth and early eleventh centuries based upon a new social order, with new needs. The thegn had changed. Instead of being a noble man of high status he had become a small local landowner or tenant. The expansion of the class from a small group of warriors in the early ninth century to a much larger class of soldiers in the late tenth century left the social theorist far behind. Although the king's thegn was a great figure, many ordinary thegns possessed far less than the five hides of land needed to be recognised as such according to conservative commentators of the time (Whitelock 1979b, p. 468). It was the growth of this mass of men which had caused so much change in the Somerset countryside. Writing in 1985, Michael Aston pointed out that there were few empty areas to colonise and warned of the danger of assuming that new settlements came into existence, especially in the east of the county (Aston 1985b). The expansion of population in the tenth century was encouraged by the extension of arable land and the production of more cereal crops. It is likely that, where crops had not been grown regularly before (as would have been the case with some areas of the new open-field), the yields available would initially have been high and this would have allowed a rapid expansion of population. The agrarian revolution of the tenth century used the existing space more efficiently. Where, perhaps, hamlets and individual farmsteads had lain amongst tracts of grazing land, now there was room for more fields and more people by packing them together more effectively. In addition, the expansion of arable increased the need for plough teams. The new field systems used the ox teams more efficiently than individual holdings could have done, relieving pressure on meadow and pasture. But there was something else which affected the lives of peasants as well as noblemen. In the tenth century men paid taxes, collected in coin by the government. England had used money for several centuries, but now large amounts of coin were circulating, as the rural economy left behind subsistence as an ideal and turned instead to markets, and the markets were mostly in towns.

6

Towns and churches

Somerset in the eighth and the ninth centuries had no towns. The royal centres, where the king might have his hall, probably consisted of the hall and its associated service buildings and nothing more. Yet activities which were typically urban at a later date, such as manufacturing and trade, took place at the king's hall, or on monastic sites. The Alfred Jewel, found in 1693, in North Petherton parish, was probably one of several related pieces made in King Alfred's time, perhaps at North Petherton or a similar site (Musgrave 1698). Metalworking was carried on at Cheddar and this is the only royal dwelling place in Somerset where a royal palace is known with certainty (Rahtz 1979, pp. 252-3). Here, a succession of wooden halls has been excavated (Rahtz 1979), along with their associated service buildings, sited on level ground, raised above likely flood level and close to the site of the Roman villa (Rahtz 1979, p. 33). The palace at Cheddar seems to have begun with a hall almost 25 metres long, placed north to south, with other smaller buildings around it. This two-storied building had a fireplace on the first floor. Built at least as early as the mid-ninth century it continued in use until c. 930 (Rahtz 1979, p. 49). It was probably here that King Alfred stayed when he entertained Guthrum and his followers after Guthrum's baptism in 878 (ASC), and the estate, together with the hall, passed to his son Edward the Elder by the terms of Alfred's will (Whitelock 1979b, pp. 334-7). The witan met in the successor hall, built around 930, on at least three occasions. The site was especially favoured as a hunting centre, since a huge tract of the Mendips was included in the estate, but may also have been a collecting point for lead – as it was to be throughout the Middle Ages.

Other royal estates almost certainly had similar halls, large enough to accommodate the king and his followers, together with all the associated lodgings, stables, barns, storehouses and workshops which would have been required. It is likely that several halls, similar to Cheddar, await discovery, particularly at Somerton and Frome. In the early days it is likely that royal houses existed and were used on most of the royal estates of ancient demesne, but by the tenth century the kings of Wessex were also kings of the English and had a wider country to cover on their travels. Yet between 934 and 1009, there are records of visits to Cheddar on three occasions, twice each to Frome, Bath and Glastonbury and once to Somerton (Hill 1981, pp. 87–91). Most other estates had become supply centres, rather than places regularly visited by the king and his court.

Throughout the period from 658 until the beginning of the tenth century it was normal for the king's court to be the centre for trade and for manufacture. As Richard Hodges has put it 'The critical phase, of course, is when the elite organisations, who have been concerned primarily with the transfer of prestige items begin to use their position to administer and manage surplus' (1982, p. 130). Ine's laws, at the beginning of the eighth century, envisaged the movement of merchants about the countryside and sought to control them (Whitelock 1979b, p. 401). By the tenth century trading was moving increasingly into the towns, which were royal creations and under royal control. As trade became too much for the king to organise and control in the countryside, the towns provided the centres where the king could continue to exploit trade and to draw profits from it.

As a child, King Alfred had visited Rome. On his travels he had seen continental towns and probably the fortifications undertaken by Charles the Bald (Hassall and Hill 1970, pp. 188–95). The latter fortified bridges on the major rivers after 862, and he ordered the rebuilding of the stone walls of Le Mans and Tours in 869 (McKitterick 1983, pp. 232–3). Fortifications were not, in any case, a new idea to the Anglo-Saxons. What was important about the works undertaken by Alfred was that they were planned as a scheme which encompassed the whole of southern England and which left no concentration of population isolated (Hill 1981, pp. 85–6). In addition, some at least of the *burhs*, as the forts were called, were planned as towns rather than as simple refuges (Campbell *et al.* 1982, pp. 152–3), suggesting that trade was recognised as important enough to be defended. Just as important as the creation of the system of *burhs* by Alfred was the maintenance and extension of the system by his successor Edward the Elder. There can be little doubt that a *burh* which was defended against the Danes was all but impregnable and the existence of an unreduced fortress in the region made it well nigh impossible for them to maintain themselves in the neigbourhood for long. The system of *burhs* worked because Alfred and his successors created a system which provided for the upkeep and defence of each fortification. Around each *burh* a number of hides were allocated to the upkeep and manning of the place, so that it has proved possible to estimate the size of each *burh* from the allocation of hides for its upkeep and defence. The survival of the 'Burghal Hidage', an administrative text which names the *burhs* and outlines the system of maintenance and defence, is good evidence of the importance attached to the system and the determination of Alfred and his heirs that it should be permanent (Hill 1969, pp. 84–92).

The *burhs* in Somerset were Axbridge, Bath, Langport, Lyng and Watchet (Hill 1969, p. 87). Axbridge, Lyng, Langport and Watchet were all linked to royal estates (Fig. 6.1). Axbridge was the *burh* for the estate at Cheddar. Medieval documents show that much of the farm land used by Axbridge residents lay in Cheddar, and the parish of Axbridge was a very small area of land, taken out of the western end of the Cheddar estate, on the edge of which the *burh* was built. Topographical analysis suggests that the *burh* lay to the south of the present town centre (Batt 1975, pp. 22–5) and the Burghal Hidage attached 400 hides to the *burh*, giving it defences of about 500 metres length and an area of 1·36 ha. We might guess that the fortified area consisted of a bank and ditch with a wooden palisade, although nothing has been found to confirm this (Aston, 1984, p. 173). The place-name 'Axbridge' is perfectly straightforward, meaning 'the

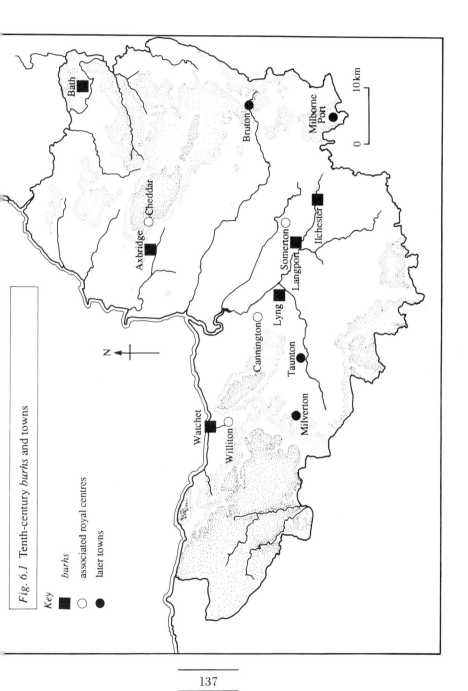

Fig. 6.1 Tenth-century *burhs* and towns

Key

■ *burhs*

○ associated royal centres

● later towns

bridge on the river Axe' (Ekwall 1960), suggesting that it was set up to guard a crossing point on the river which gave access to Cheddar for those coming from the south-west, as well as covering the route along the foot of the Mendips from the west.

Langport lies on a small promontory on the western end of the high ground upon which Somerton stands, beside the river Parrett. It guards the approach to Somerton from the west, at a crossing point which leads to other royal estates at Curry and towards Taunton. Here an earth rampart cut off the burh from the mainland, while the river and the marshes provided defence on the west (Aston 1984, p. 182).

Lyng also lies on a promontory, this time closing the road which led to Taunton and at the same time complementing the first fort built by Alfred on Athelney, which is only 500 metres to the north-east. The Burghal hidage gives only 100 hides for the support of Lyng, which allows for only short defences. These crossed the peninsula on which the modern village stands, making an economical defence. The narrow gap between the two forts was important because a river, the Yeo, flowed through it, while the river Tone ran close to the eastern side of the fort on Athelney (Williams 1970). Asser remarked that a causeway had been built between the two sites 'by protracted labour' and 'a formidable fortress of elegant workmanship was set up by the command of the king at the western end of the causeway' (Keynes and Lapidge 1983, p. 103). The construction seems to have been a fortified bridge, giving access to the king's most secure stronghold.

At Watchet, the Iron Age hillfort has been suggested as the site of the burh (Aston 1984, p. 193). The site at Watchet clearly needed to be well defended and to be so sited that good views of the sea were available. The greatest danger was of attack from the sea. In 917 a pirate fleet ravaged the south-western parts of Britain. The king had ordered the coast to be guarded but 'they landed secretly by night on two separate occasions, once east of Watchet and again at Porlock, and on each occasion the English struck them so that only those few escaped who swam out to the ships'. Probably by 988 the burh was in some disarray since 'Watchet was ravaged' and the same thing happened in 997 (ASC).

Bath had been part of Mercia for many centuries and probably did not pass into the control of the kings of Wessex until the latter part of King Alfred's reign. The charter for North Stoke (S. 265), was a grant to the monastic church of St Peter in Bath and a charter of 796 was dated from 'the celebrated town . . . æt Bathum' (S. 149). The town was fortified as a *burh*, by using its Roman fortifications and the allowance in the Burghal Hidage of 1,000 hides reflects the size of the fortifications and the area it was meant to defend.

A mint was established at Bath soon after the turn of the century, suggesting that it was already in use as a major trading centre (Grinsell 1973) and Barry Cunliffe has suggested that the town may have been replanned and rebuilt in the tenth century after the model of Winchester and other towns in Wessex (Cunliffe 1984a). It emerged in the tenth century as the major commercial centre for the southern part of Gloucestershire and northern Somerset. The Anglo-Saxon charters of the tenth century for this region show that roads to Bath were already important in the middle of the century and it is likely that the Fosse Way had never fallen out of use. In 970 it was *fosse streat* to the south of the town and was also the *stræt* to the north of the town in 957 (S. 777; S. 643), but many other local roads are also mentioned in charters of the tenth century for the district around Bath. Roads are mentioned in the charters for Weston and North Stoke, on the western side of Bath, to the north of the river Avon and Stanton Prior, Marksbury, Priston, Corston and Evesty all use roads as parts of boundaries (Fig. 6.2). Nearly all these roads run to Bath, showing how much it dominated the communications and the trade of the north eastern part of Somerset.

Axbridge was subsequently developed as a town, as was Langport, but at Lyng this did not occur, probably because it was too isolated to be a trading place. Watchet was also abandoned and the town grew up in the valley below. Other sites were also exploited as towns and, during the tenth century, Somerset had more urban centres than anywhere else in the South-West. Bruton, Ilchester, Langport, Milborne Port, Milverton and Taunton as well as Bath and Axbridge all had burgesses in 1086 (DB) but mints at Crewkerne, South Cadbury, South Petherton and Watchet indicate a degree of urban development at some time in the tenth century. In addition, Frome

F

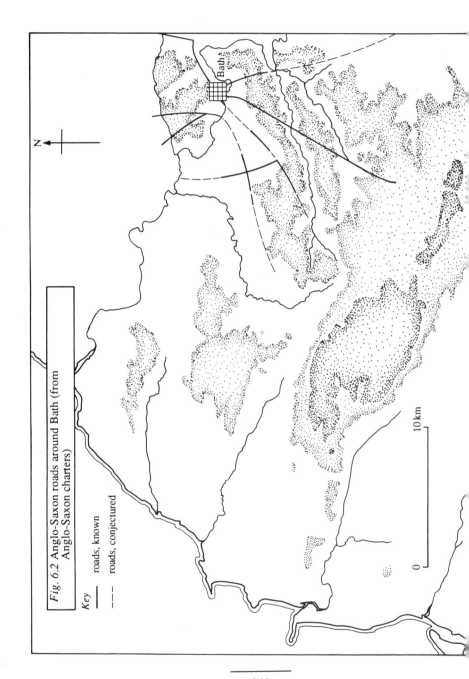

Fig. 6.2 Anglo-Saxon roads around Bath (from Anglo-Saxon charters)

Key
—— roads, known
- - - roads, conjectured

Bath

N

0   10 km

and Ilminster had markets in 1086. Clearly the criteria used to define towns in the tenth century cannot be uniformly applied since very few places could meet them all (Biddle 1976). Almost all the 'towns' were royal property and most were established at the centre of royal estates. This was certainly the case for Bruton, Crewkerne, Frome, Milborne Port, Milverton and South Petherton. Axbridge, Watchet, Ilchester and Langport were all within royal estates, but sited away from the central place. Some of these towns still shows signs of planning in their street patterns. Milborne Port has been suggested as a possible example and it seems very likely that a town was deliberately founded outside the king's residence at Kingsbury Regis, which lies just a little to the north of the present town. The recently discovered hall site of the tenth/eleventh century just behind the church probably related to the town or the church and not to the king's residence (Fig. 6.3). Bath had not been the centre of a royal estate, but the borough which existed there in 1086 belonged in part to the king (DB 1, 31). This suggests that the king had put money into the venture, although he was not the major owner, since other men had jurisdiction over ninety other burgesses. Barry Cunliffe's 'tentative reconstruction' of late Saxon Bath also shows a planned town centre, as one might expect with a commercial undertaking of this size (Cunliffe 1984a, p. 348, fig. 115). Taunton and Ilminster were not royal property in the tenth century. Taunton belonged to the bishop of Winchester and Ilminster to the Abbey of Muchelney. At Taunton we may assume that the king had granted a privilege to the bishop which allowed him to found and profit from a borough and at Ilminster he had granted a market as a source of income to the monastery.

The king emerges as the agent who controlled and encouraged the development of the boroughs and markets of Somerset. The unique distribution of small mints, and, by implication, small towns in Somerset and Wiltshire has been explained by Dr David Hill as an act of deliberate policy by the king, seeking to maximise his income in an area where grants to the church, in particular had reduced his revenue (Hill 1978, p. 222).

Such a policy does not imply that Somerset was especially rich in the tenth century. The mints themselves were small and the later distribution of burgesses suggests that all the towns were modest in size and hence in wealth, with only Bath approaching

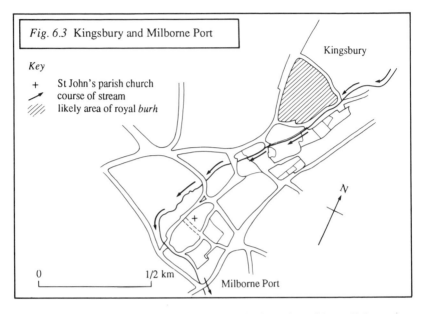

Fig. 6.3 Kingsbury and Milborne Port

Key
+ St John's parish church
↗ course of stream
/// likely area of royal *burh*

Kingsbury

N

0   1/2 km

Milborne Port

the importance of the county boroughs in other shires. Ilchester, which had 107 burgesses in 1086 (DB 1, 10), was the most important urban centre south of the Mendips. There were a number of reasons for this. It benefited from its position as the most important point of trade in the county, as it had in Roman times. The Fosse Way was of the utmost importance as a trade route. To the south it led to Exeter. D. M. Metcalf has demonstrated the importance of seaports as centres of overseas trade in the later tenth century, and the production of the bulk of the coinage can be traced to these towns. Furthermore, the composition of hoards and the distribution of the output of mints demonstrates that the coinage quickly circulated throughout the whole country, suggesting that the long distance element in trade was extremely important (Metcalf 1978). As well as benefiting from trade along the Fosse, Ilchester was also well placed for distribution into central Somerset and it controlled access overland from Wiltshire. Early in the eleventh century its mint had been forced to retreat to Cadbury Castle for safety as did similar mints at Dorchester and Chichester (Hill 1978), but this was only a temporary state of affairs and it continued to be the principal centre for control of long-distance trade. Milborne

Port, with fifty-six burgesses in 1086, was probably also involved in part of the same long-distance distribution.

During the latter part of the tenth century and the first half of the eleventh the Anglo-Saxon Chronicle records the payment of vast sums of money in tribute to the Danes. Over £250,000 was paid out. John Gillingham has recently challenged the view that the Old English state could command such resources in taxation (Gillingham 1989), but the calculations of numismatists suggest that the quantity of coinage in circulation would support burdens of this kind, especially if, as has been suggested, the level of English trade was such that a substantial balance of trade surplus existed (Metcalf 1978; 1982, p. 204). A deep depression would have ensued if such sums had been insupportable as silver became scarce, but the evidence of Domesday Book is that the economy of Somerset had expanded considerably during the tenth and the first half of the eleventh centuries. It is against such a background that we must view the towns of the county. Although they were royal creations, they depended ultimately on the countryside which provided the produce and the customers. This was how the king tried to assure himself of a share of the prosperity of his people. The small towns of Somerset, then unusually close together and early in their growth, survive to this day. Other towns were founded at a later date, mostly in the century and a half after the Norman Conquest, but the royal foundations of the tenth century provided the skeleton around which the flesh was later wrapped.

The church

The profound changes in the nature of the Anglo-Saxon countryside of the tenth and the eleventh centuries inevitably affected the secular church. The changes which took place reflected not only the expansion of population but also the changing relationships among the ruling elite in Old English society. But just as the changes in secular society were based solidly upon the framework of landownership and personal relationships of an earlier age, so the changes in the church represented no sudden break with the past, but rather a change which took the existing structure as its base.

Firstly, Somerset became a diocese in 909, with the bishopric based at Wells. This was part of a general reorganisation of pastoral responsibilities in the South-West, which also involved the foundation of a bishopric for Devon and Cornwall, undertaken by Edward the Elder when Asser, the Bishop of Sherborne died (Stenton 1947, p. 433). Wells was chosen for the seat of the bishop, although the reasons for the choice are not known. It seems likely that the sacred nature of the site, as well as its position convenient to the bulk of the royal estates and to communications eastward, influenced the decision.

The chief endowment of the new bishopric was the land of Wells itself, for which the Cathedral possessed no 'book', suggesting that it already belonged to the church there in 909 (Liber Albus). Such a generous endowment thus cost the king little, since it was not taken out of his existing lands. Chew Magna was probably granted to the bishop at the time of the foundation and some estates were passed on from Sherborne (S. 380 of 899 × 909 and S. 262 of 766; Edwards 1988, pp. 259–60). By 1066, the bishop and the cathedral owned 223 hides of land, an area which provided a substantial endowment to support the bishop's administration and the cathedral and its services. The construction of a cathedral probably took place soon after the foundation of the diocese and it was built close to the ancient Christian site beside the holy well of St Andrew (Rodwell 1980).

The creation of the diocese undoubtedly coincided with the growth in the numbers of churches under the control of the bishop. A hierarchy of ecclesiastical lordship existed which it would not be too fanciful to see as reflecting the emerging hierarchy of lordship in secular society. But the dominant role in the countryside, at least in formal organisation, still lay with the minster churches (Whitelock 1979b, p. 431). Many survived the upheavals of the ninth century (Blair 1988a, p. 3) and, in some, the collegiate life may well have survived into the twelfth century. There is no clear agreement as to which churches were minsters, or, indeed, which churches actually were in existence in Somerset by the middle of the eleventh century. Neither is it at all clear when most churches were founded. Even in the Middle Ages false trails were laid. A charter of Glastonbury Abbey and even a letter from the Pope quoted by William of Malmesbury purport to show that the churches of Middlezoy, East Brent, Moorlinch, Shapwick, Street, Butleigh and Pilton were all in existence by 725 anu objects of concern to the Pope in the tenth century. Some of them may have been, but Glastonbury Abbey muddied the water for us by doctoring the Pope's letter at a later date (S. 250; Edwards 1988, p. 37; Whitelock 1979b, p. 895).

As we have seen already, many of the minster churches were early foundations and this is especially likely for the royal estates. By the tenth century the evidence for many of these sites becomes much firmer. The gazetteer at the end of this chapter lists over twenty possible minster sites and the association with the centres of large and important estates is obvious. Collegiality may still have existed at some of the minsters at the time of the Norman Conquest. At Crewkerne, between 1272 and 1282, the rectory was divided into three 'portions', one each for the rector, the deacon and the sub-deacon (Dunning 1978, pp. 28–9). Clearly, the living had been held undivided until that time and the three officers look like the remnants of a college or guild of priests. The chapelries of Crewkerne, at Misterton, Wayford, Seaborough and Eastham did not become independent until the mid-thirteenth century, but there is no certainty that they existed in the tenth or the eleventh centuries. The tenants of the estates at Wayford and Oathill were obliged to attend the mother church at Crewkerne on 24 August, the date of the feast of St Bartholemew, to whom Crewkerne was dedicated. At St Decuman's there was still a Dean in the mid-twelfth century, presumably the survivor of the college of clerks which had once existed there (Dunning 1985, p. 165). The church at Kilmersdon retained control of the chapel of Ashwick until 1413, when the chapel gained its own burial ground (Maxwell-Lyte and Dawes 1934). Ashwick had been an estate of the Abbey of Bath in the tenth century. At Shapwick, the chapels at Ashcot, Catcott, and Edington never escaped from the control of the mother church, probably because the rectory was impropriated by the Abbey of Glastonbury.

The most conservative of minster churches was the Head Minster, Wells itself. Here the mother church did not allow the creation of new parish churches within its estates, and, since the ancient estate of Wells survived intact into the Norman period, parish churches were absent from a large tract of countryside. Only Wookey and Westbury became parishes in the post-

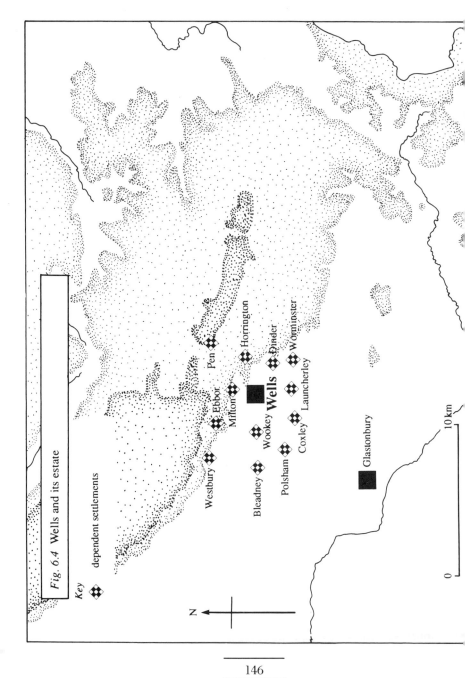

Fig. 6.4 Wells and its estate

Key

dependent settlements

Hornington
Worminster
Dinder
Pen
Launcherley
Ebbor
Wells
Milton
Wookey
Coxley
Westbury
Bleadney
Polsham
Glastonbury

N

0   10 km

Conquest period. Other villages remained chapelries of the mother church of St Cuthbert (Fig. 6.4).

Among the churches referred to as minsters there was clearly a hierarchy of age. Pitminster, for example, may preserve the name of the founder of the church. The estate was certainly not a central place, so the foundation of the church may have occurred after the estate was detached. But there were also many churches which were not minsters. The driving force behind their foundation was probably the break-up of estates into smaller units, which encouraged landowners to build churches for themselves and their dependants as a sign of their independence. How soon such churches obtained burial rights we do not know. It is clear from the Laws of Edgar (959–63) that old minsters, churches with graveyards and churches without graveyards were in existence, and also causing enough problems to require legislation (Whitelock 1979b, p. 431). King Edgar's legislation was aimed at thegns with churches on their bookland. These were the people who were founding the churches of the mid-tenth century and, thereby, appropriating a part of the tithes of their minster church. It seems likely that this was one motive in the foundation of a church, since the tithes might then be diverted to the thegn's own use, but status was also important. At a time when the thegnage was expanding rapidly and becoming a military class, social mobility was clearly high. In such circumstances marks of rank became important. The 'Compilation on status' of 1002–23 tells us that a ceorl who prospered might become a thegn if he had five hides of land of his own, a bell house, a fortified gatehouse and a seat and special office in the king's hall. One version of the text adds 'a church and kitchen', suggesting that the church was seen as the typical adjunct of a thegn by the early eleventh century (Whitelock 1979a, p. 468). The differing contents of different versions of the text also highlight the fluidity of the position of the thegn. The texts seem to look back to a time of stability, when relationships were clearly understood, emphasising the sense of change when the compilations were made. It would seem, therefore, that we should look for the emergence of independent churches with graveyards on secular estates, or on those church estates which were isolated. At West Camel, for example the land was granted to the Abbey of Muchelney and the remains of a cross shaft from the village might suggest a pre-Conquest church. Rowberrow, on the other hand, was almost certainly a secular estate, although not recorded in the Domesday Book, as was Lullington in 1066 (DB 5, 51).

In suggesting that Alston Sutton may have had a chapel without a graveyard by 1066, I have implied that it was an offshoot of a church with a graveyard, since the inhabitants of the new estate needed to be buried somewhere (Costen 1991b). The church in question might have been Wedmore or possibly Upper Weare, to which Alston Sutton was ecclesiastically attached in the post-Conquest period. At Alston Sutton, the chapel never gained a graveyard and yet the priest had the tithes of the manor in the Middle Ages. At Crewkerne, on the other hand, the subsidiary chapels at Misterton, Seaborough and Wayford continued to bury their dead at Crewkerne into modern times. At Taunton, many daughter churches already existed by the time of the Norman Conquest. Many a parish church must have started as a chapel without a burial ground, owned by the thegn who built it and who collected the tithes. Unfortunately we are only rarely conscious of when this was the case, or where a church was founded after the Norman Conquest. However, the implication of the archeological finds at places which were modest settlements in the eleventh century is that churches were very common and that the majority of communities had a place of worship close at hand. The development of the rural church was made possible by the growing wealth of the countryside, but the pattern it took was the result of the demands of the rural elite, for whom a church beside the hall was a sign of status as well as something which served to bind the peasantry more closely to them. At a time when the reorganisation of fields and villages was bringing the rural dweller into ever closer dependence upon the lord, the control of the local church served to emphasise the dominance of the lord in the community and also provided him with an additional way of exploiting the peasants' surplus, since he collected the tithes.

Monasteries were another aspect of this control of the countryside, but the motivation which led to their refoundation and development was probably opposed by nobility when the movement first began. There is little to suggest that Glastonbury had survived as a working monastery into the tenth century. It seems likely that it had become, by *c.* 940, little more than a collegiate church (Knowles 1963, p. 696). William of Malmesbury thought that the monastery had been without monks from the time of the Danish raids into the area in the reign of Alfred (Hamilton 1870, p. 196). It is difficult to imagine that the monastery had been able to survive a war which had forced Alfred himself to retreat to the marshes. Quite apart from the problems posed by war, the monasteries also suffered from the attentions of the English nobility and even the crown. Estates granted to the monasteries were either alienated or were seized by the king so that they could be used to meet the king's military needs (Fleming 1985). There is some evidence to show that that this happened to Glastonbury. A part of the Brent estate was granted to the monastery by a charter of 973 (S. 793). There is no documentation to show when the estate was granted away or whether it was simply taken. Its return made the Brent estate complete once more. It is likely that the estates of Glastonbury Abbey were smaller than the number of surviving charters would suggest and the loss of lands was probably the major reason for the collapse of monastic life (Costen 1991a, forthcoming), since without income the regular monastic life could not be supported. Ultimately, the viability of the monastic life depended upon the stability of society. Monks could survive in a dangerous world, providing that all sides in any political struggle recognised that the monks were outside the politics of the day. Generally that had been true of the early Anglo-Saxon monarchies, but invasion by pagans and the weakening of bonds within English society inevitably brought a collapse. It seems that all the monasteries had ceased to function as monasteries by 940, even those such as Athelney and Shaftesbury which could claim King Alfred himself as their founder.

The revival came as the result of the work of St Dunstan. Born in Somerset, possibly at Baltonsborough, a Glastonbury estate (Robinson 1923, p. 82), he came from an ecclesiastical family, numbering Ælfheah the bishop of Winchester and the bishop of Lichfield among his kin, as well as being a relative of King Athelstan (Robinson 1919). He was probably intended for a career in the church and, after an early education at Glastonbury, he received further training from Athelm, who became Archbishop of Canterbury in 923 (Knowles 1963, p. 696). He then moved to the court of King Athelstan where in 939, after a period as chaplain to his uncle at Winchester, he became a chaplain or counsellor to King Edmund. It was while he was at King Edmund's court that he began to promote the idea of monastic reform and, as a result, was threatened with exile because of the dissension he was stirring up within the court. However, in 940, King Edmund had a narrow escape from death while hunting on the Mendips above Cheddar and, in thanks to God, decided to make Dunstan Abbot of Glastonbury (Stubbs 1874, pp. 24–5).

Both Dunstan and his enemies must have been aware of the movement for monastic reform which was gathering pace on the continent. They must also have realised that a resumption of monastic properties which had been alienated was a part of the reforming process. This was what had stirred up hostility at the King's court and made the chronicler of Dunstan's life feel that Edmund's decision could only be explained as a miracle. Dunstan set out to reform his monastery and to reintroduce the monastic life. Although his ecclesiatical career was not without its vagaries, Glastonbury was successfully rebuilt. Dunstan's contemporaries, Æthelwold of Winchester and Oswald, archbishop of York, were equally important in other parts of the country. As with the reform movement on the continent, the English reformers were driven by a desire to establish a regular life which was uniform, or as uniform as possible, and in 970, by a national agreement at the Council of Winchester, they adopted a version of the Rule of St Benedict known as the *Regularis Concordia* (Symons 1953). This agreement made it possible for a degree of regularity to exist throughout the growing English monastic movement. In Somerset, Athelney and Muchelney may have been refounded or reformed around 970, while Bath was effected before that date. A charter of 956 (S. 610) granted land at Tidenham in Gloucestershire to the monastery of Bath and named its abbot, Wulfgar.

At a purely physical level the first effect of the reforms was the rebuilding of the monasteries. St Dunstan is credited with the rebuilding of Glastonbury and he certainly began the work which led to the construction of the monastery and the enlargement of the existing church in order to make the plan conform to the normal monastic enclosure pattern (Radford 1981, p. 119). The stone buildings of the convent were probably the first stone domestic structures erected at the monastery and may mark a new era in building. The stone for the building work may have come from a quarry at West Pennard which was in existence during the tenth century (S. 236). At Bath, the church was probably of stone by the second half of the tenth century but nothing survives of the monastery of that period (Cunliffe 1984a, pp. 352–3).

The impact of the reforms was twofold. After the initial opposition to the movement, some of the landowning classes joined in the reform movement with enthusiasm. It was from among their ranks that the monks were drawn. With the tenth-century kings leading the way, they gave grants of land to the monasteries. At Glastonbury, between 943 and 956 – the year when Dunstan went into exile (Stenton 1947, p. 442) – land at Mells, North Wootton, East Pennard, Doulting, Whatley and Panbough, amounting to seventy hides, is recorded as having come to the community (Finberg 1964, nos 445, 458, 469, 461, 452 and 470). By 1066 the Abbey had acquired 416 hides in Somerset alone (DB, chapter 7). Glastonbury Abbey was outstandingly successful in its pursuit of land. Other monasteries – St Peter's at Bath, Muchelney and Athelney – also benefited from noble generosity so that by 1086 these monasteries held between 19 and 20 per cent of the land in the county (DB; Darby and Welldon-Finn 1967). The great churches of Wells and Winchester also had extensive holdings and about a quarter of the county was thus in ecclesiastical hands. As landlords the monasteries were little different from other landowners (Costen 1991a, forthcoming), except that they did not exploit their estates as efficiently as laymen, but the extent of their estates meant that a large area of land previously available for redistribution by grant or inheritance, was permanently removed from circulation. Those estates which stayed in the hands of monasteries were not divided as the result of inheritance practice, so that church lands tended to be concentrated in larger units, allowing the growth of larger field systems and villages.

The spiritual dimension of the monastic expansion is less easy to define. The estates granted were the physical expression of the spiritual relationship between the local aristocracy and the monks. The monks offered a spiritual service to the lay community which they valued. The monastic life offered a standard of behaviour against which the rest of society could be measured and men looked with approval upon a puritanical authority which would impose that standard upon others. Hence Dunstan's role at King Eadwig's coronation feast, when he alone dared to drag the dissolute king back to the table from the embraces of a mother and daughter (Rollason 1989, p. 170)! In the observance of the regular life, the laity saw a guarantee that God and the saints would be approached on behalf of the community, so that the invisible and the visible worlds could exist in harmony. This was the monks' work – their justification for support. The close connection between those two worlds was epitomised by the possession and use of relics. Glastonbury claimed to possess the relics of many saints, including St Patrick, St David and St Bridget, as well as many others, and William of Malmesbury presented a long list when he wrote his history (Scott 1981, pp. 69–71). After the refoundation, Glastonbury pursued a policy of collecting relics and that may have included the translation of local relics to Glastonbury itself, as well as the purchase or receipt of gifts of relics from further afield. Relics conferred power on their possessor, both because of the prestige of their ownership and because of the power of the saint, who drew pilgrims and who gave spiritual power and protection by his privileged position in the unseen world. Measured on any scale, the spiritual power of Glastonbury was overwhelming. It is not surprising that in the tenth century four of the bishops of Wells came from Glastonbury Abbey, while five of the six archbishops of Canterbury after Dunstan came from the same community (Carley 1988, p. 12: St Alphege came from Bath Abbey). Such a privileged position did not mean the end of opposition or enmity, but the community were better able to resist it than before. Both kings and noblemen could, and did, despoil the church on occasion and the gift of estates often slowed down and even stopped altogether (Keynes 1980, p. 181). On occasion it was necessary to call upon even the Pope and his threat of spiritual penalties. This expedient was actually used against Ealdorman Ælfric quite soon after the Glastonbury reforms, when Pope John XII (d. 965) wrote:

> We have learnt from the report of certain faithful people that you commit many injuries against the church of Mary the holy

Mother of God, which is called Glastonbury, and in your greedy cupidity have seized estates and villages from its rightful ownership, and you are constantly harmful to it because you constantly cling to a dwelling place close to the same place. It would have been fitting, when you became its neighbour, that the holy church of God might have greatly benefited by your support, and have been enriched in possessions by means of your help; but what is abominable, it is impoverished by your opposition and humiliated by your oppression. Pope John went on to threaten excommunication (Whitelock 1979b, p. 895).

In 995, the monastery of Muchelney related how it had granted an estate to laymen for three lives (S. 884) and how the leasees wrongfully gained a charter for the land and refused to return it. They regained the land only with difficulty by going to the shire court and obtaining judgement from ealdormen and bishops.

Despite its great spiritual advantages Somerset did not stay long at the centre of religious affairs. By the eleventh century, Glastonbury, although rich and famous, had begun to slip back with a succession of incompetent abbots (Carley 1988, p. 13). Religious power and authority tended to follow the king and his court, and by the early eleventh century political power had moved away.

A gazetteer of possible church sites in late Anglo-Saxon Somerset

(*Monastic sites are noted in this list, but not discussed.*)

Aller: Aller was the site of Guthrum's baptism in 878 (ASC). Architectural evidence (Foster 1987). See also Dunning (1974), p. 69 (VCH hereafter), for the possibility that Aller was a minster.

Athelney: A monastic site.

Alston Sutton: There may have been a chapel without a graveyard here. See Costen (1991b).

Banwell: Named as a minster (Keynes and Lapidge (1983), p. 97). In addition the place name may come from OE **bana**, 'a slayer' + OE **wiell**, 'a spring', perhaps a reference to the use of a pool or spring for the administration of the ordeal by water. Judicial ordeals were religious ceremonies in the

Old English period and were normally administered by clerks. Architectural evidence, see Foster (1987).

Bath: A monastic site.

Bedminster: Place name, OE **Beda**, a personal name + **mynster**, probably commemorates the name of a priest at Bedminster. Since the site was ancient demesne it is unlikely to be the name of a secular founder. See (DB 1, 7). Since the priest held one hide in 1086 this may indicate that this was a minster church.

Bradford on Tone: The DB entry for Taunton (DB 2, 2) tells us that the lords of certain lands, which were part of the Taunton manor, were obliged to be buried at Taunton. This was a sign of the superior rights of the mother church at Taunton, but the fact that the rest of the inhabitants were not buried at Taunton implies that there was a churchyard available locally. Other places named in the same Domesday Book entry will be described as 'by inference'.

Brent: There was a priest holding land in 1086, 1·5 hides (DB 8, 33), probable church.

Bruton: William of Malmesbury's Life of St Aldhelm refers to two churches at Bruton in the late seventh century. Bruton was ancient demesne. Probably a minster.

West Camel: Architectural (Foster 1987).

Cannington: (DB 16, 3) A church and 2·5 virgates of land and on ancient demesne, probably a minster church.

Carhampton: (DB 16, 6) One and a half hides of land and on ancient demesne, probably a minster.

Cheddar: The will of King Alfred (Keynes and Lapidge 1983, pp. 173–78). It was ancient demesne (see DB 1, 2). See also chapter 4 above. Also S. 806 of 968 speaks of the 'community' at Cheddar, suggesting a comunity of priests. In 1068 it was *Ceodder mynster* (Liber Albus II, fo. 246). A minster church.

Cheddon Fitzpaine: By inference from Taunton.

Upper Cheddon: Inference from Taunton.

Cheriton: The place-name is OE **cirice**, 'a church' + **tūn**.

Chew Stoke: Architectural evidence (Foster 1987).

Chewton: (DB 1, 29) The church is mentioned and held half a hide of land. It may have been a minster, since it was on a large royal estate.

Chillington: VCH, vol. IV, p. 132 says of Chillington '(it) bears all the traces of a prehistoric site'. It is unlikely that the site would have been chosen at a late date if this is the case. However, this is a very tentative inclusion in the gazetteer.

Congresbury: Asser (Keynes and Lapidge 1983), see above for Banwell. The connection with the Celtic saint Cungar is also explored in Chapter 4.

Crewkerne: (DB 1, 20) The church of Crewkerne is mentioned (DB 12, 1). It held 10 hides at Misterton, which is OE **mynster** + **tūn**. It was undoubtedly a minster.

North Curry: (DB 1, 19) A church with 3 hides of land. Probably a minster.

Curry Rivel: (DB 16, 11) This was a church with half a hide. Whether it was a minster is doubtful, though possible, since this was ancient demesne.

Doulting: St Aldhelm built a wooden church here according to his 'Life' (Hamilton 1870).

Ford: Inference from Taunton, see above.

Frome: Church of St John. St Aldhelm is recorded as founding a monastery here; see above, Chapter 4 (Hamilton 1870. Also DB 1, 8). The church had an estate of 8 carucates. Architectural (Foster 1987).

Glastonbury: Monastic site.

Halse: Inference from Taunton, see above.

Heathfield: Inference from Taunton, see above.

Hele: Inference from Taunton, see above.

Henstridge: Architectural (Foster 1987).

Hillfarance: Inference from Taunton, see above.

Holcombe: Architectural (Foster 1987).

Holford: Inference from Taunton, see above.

Ilchester: St Andrew Northover (DB 8, 37) three hides of land. This was a minster church. See VCH, vol. III, p. 228. The ancient parish of Northover represents this estate.

Ilminster: Place-name, the minster on the Ile (a river name).

Kelston: Architectural (Foster 1987).

Keynsham: Architectural (Foster 1987 and Lowe *et al.* 1987).

Kilmersdon: (DB 16, 14) Half a hide of land, possible minster church.

Long Ashton: (DB 5, 34) A church and one virgate of land.

Lullington: Architectural (Foster 1987).

Maidenbrooke: Inference from Taunton, see above.

Maperton: Architectural (Foster 1987).

Marston Magna: Herringbone masonry cut by a Norman window (pers. comment, Mr M. Aston).

Martock: Suggested minster (VCH, vol. IV, p. 102).

Michael Church: Place-name, *michaeliscerce* (DB 46, 13).

Milborne Port: Church of St John (DB 1, 10) a church with one hide. Architectural (Foster 1987). A minister church.

Milverton: (DB 16, 4) A church with one virgate and one furlong.

Muchelney: A monastery.

Nether Stowey: (VCH, vol. V, p. 197) Suggested as a minster church site.

Norton Fitzwarren: Inference from Taunton, see above.

Nunney: Architectural (Foster 1987).

Nynehead: Inference from Taunton, see above.

Oake: Inference from Taunton, see above.

East Pennard: Place-name (S. 503 of 955), Pengeard Mynster.

North Petherton: The Church of St Mary (DB 16, 7) a church and three virgates of land.

South Petherton: (DB 16, 5) A church and one hide of land. The royal estate was ancient demesne. A probable minster.

'Pignes': Exon Domesday shows that this place had a church, since it says 'a priest of this village's church' (DB, see p. 331, notes).

Pitminster: Place-name, OE pers. name **Pippa** + **mynster**.

Porlock: Architectural (Foster 1987).

Rowberrow: Architectural (Foster 1987).

Shapwick: Field archaeology (Costen 1991b); also inference from the size of the post-Domesday holding of the church (Costen 1989, pp. 73–5).

Shepton Mallet: Architectural (Foster 1987).

Shopnoller: Inference from Taunton, see above.

Somerton: Possible Anglo-Saxon chapel at Somerton Erlegh (Collinson 1791, III, p. 186).

Stogumber: Church of St Mary (DB 16, 2). A Church and two hides of land, probable minster.

North Stoke: Tentatively suggested as a pre-Conquest site. The church stands beside a spring and the chancel and nave are not in line. This suggests that the chancel may preserve an older alignment, typical of Anglo-Saxon churches, where the eastward orientation is not always followed rigorously.

Stoke St Mary: Inference from Taunton, see above.

Taunton: (DB 2, 1) The customary dues owed to Taunton included Peter's Pence and Church Scot. It was clearly a minster.

Tolland: Inference from Taunton, see above.

Weare: Inference from Alston Sutton, see above.

Wedmore: By inference, since this was the place where the chrism was loosened for Guthrum in 878. This was a religious ceremony and so probably took place in a church.

Wells: Chosen as bishop's seat in 909. Archaeological (Rodwell 1982).

Whitchurch: Place-name, OE **hwite** + **circe**, 'white church', probably because the building was limewashed.

Yatton: (DB 6, 14) A church and a hide of land, this may be a minster.

Yeovil: The will of Wynflaed, *c.* 950, has a gift for her soul from Chinnock to the value of half a pound for Yeovil (Whitelock 1930, p. 11).

7

'Domesday Book and beyond'

Castles and lands

We do not know when and how the first Normans entered Somerset after William the Conqueror's success in the southeast of Britain, but in the spring of 1067 William returned to Normandy taking with him a crowd of hostages, which included Æthelnoth, the Abbot of Glastonbury (ASC). He remained a captive in Normandy until his deposition in 1078 (Carley 1988, p. 13). One motive for his continued detention must have been the need to control a monastery which was the richest in the country, with an income in 1086 of £827 a year (Carley 1988, p. 14). The Anglo-Saxon Chronicle tells us that William found it necessary to besiege Exeter early in 1068, when the town revolted, and, since it could not be quickly captured by a siege, compromised to the extent that it was not looted or taxed more heavily after surrendering (Stenton 1947, p. 593). Later that year the sons of King Harold arrived from Ireland with a pirate host and after being repulsed at Bristol sailed down the Somerset coast, landed and fought a battle, which they evidently lost, despite killing Eadnoth the Staller (ASC). King Harold's mother, Gytha, had been at Exeter, before retiring first to Flatholme and then to St Omer, so it may well be that the Exeter rebellion and the landing on the coast were connected to a belief that, with so much land in the South-West, the House of Godwine might still

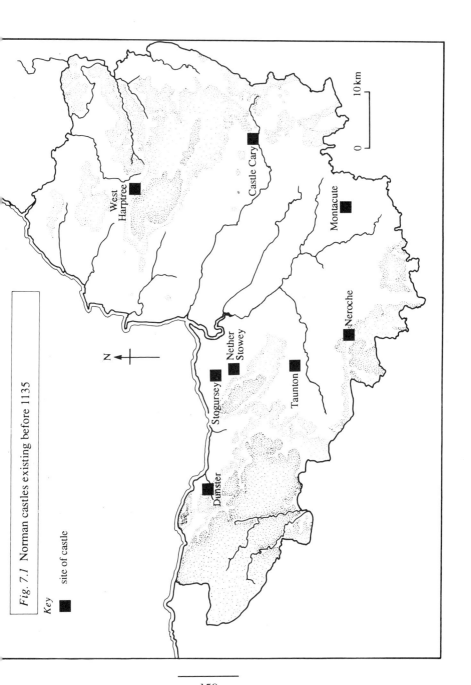

Fig. 7.1 Norman castles existing before 1135

Key

■ site of castle

10 km

West Harptree

Castle Cary

Montacute

Neroche

Stogursey

Nether Stowey

Taunton

Dunster

N

159

hope for support there (Stafford 1989, pp. 104–5). One response by the Normans to the obvious dangers of revolt and invasion from the West was to build castles (Fig. 7.1). They were major tools of the Conquest, used in England to provide strongpoints to control the countryside, on roads and at fords, and in towns to secure their obedience. The castle at Montacute had been built before the revolt in the South-West and withstood attack by local people from Somerset and Dorset in 1068 (Page 1911), suggesting that there may have been either some local sympathy with the sons of Harold, or that the heavy exactions of the Normans had already had an impact on local people. In any case, a siege of the castle suggests that there were still Englishmen capable of bearing arms, probably local landholders who had not been involved in the Battle of Hastings. The siege was raised by the Bishop of Coutances, one of the biggest landholders in the shire by 1086.

The Castle at Montacute was constructed on St Michael's Hill, a steep conical hill, made steeper by being cut away (Dunning 1974, p. 215). Probably the very first castle was of wood, given the short time available for its construction, before the revolt and siege. The site was clearly chosen because the hill was available, but it was so positioned, near the old Ham Hill hillfort, that it was close to the Fosse Way, running down to Exeter. In addition it was only a few miles south of Ilchester and within easy striking distance of the routes through Sherborne to Crewkerne and from Ilchester south to Dorchester. The castle at Dunster was built by William de Mohun, also during the Conqueror's reign, probably in response to the invasion by Harold's sons, and so placed that it could provide cover for the royal estates along the coast at Carhampton and Williton.

Castles needed an infrastructure upon which to depend; they did not stand isolated in the countryside. By 1086, the castle of Montacute, standing in the manor of Bishopston, was supported by lands held by a group of knights, Drogo, Bretel and Duncan, who each had one hide (DB 19, 86). They were some of the closest of the Count's supporters. They oversaw the castle guard, taking turns at supervision of the building and they were aided by porters, who also held land (DB 19, 38). The senior supporters of the Count also held extensive estates as his vassals, in order to make sure of their loyalty. Robert of Mortain probably also built the castle at Neroche during William's reign (Davison 1972). Here the castle stood on the escarpment, looking down over the forest towards Taunton, in Robert's manor of Staple. A simple defence was built at a very early stage after the Conquest using an existing enclosure which was later replaced by a motte and bailey castle. In the west of the county the castle at Stogursey may have been in existence as early as 1090, when it was mentioned by Oderic Vitalis. If this is the case, then it too may have started as a castle designed to control the English as well as to protect the land at the mouth of the river Parrett from external attack.

Castles were imposed upon the countryside in order to control it and they provided a counterweight to the towns which were potentially dangerous to the Normans, since they were often defensible and difficult to capture – although it is noteworthy that not a single early castle was built in a Somerset town. However, the period when castles were needed to protect the Normans against the English was probably quite short. Montacute castle had lost its military significance by 1102, when the manor and the castle were granted for the foundation of the Cluniac priory of Montacute (SRS 8, 1894, p. 119). Although other castles were built during the century after the Norman Conquest (Renn 1973), they resulted from the concerns of individual landholders, especially as they took part in politics in the early years of the twelfth century. This is well illustrated by the events at the start of William Rufus's reign, when Odo of Bayeux and William of St Calais led a rebellion against the new king, during which the Bishop of Coutances and Robert of Mowbray burnt Bath and moved on Ilchester before they were stopped (Poole 1955, pp. 100–1). A similar story occurred at the start of Stephen's reign. As the revolt against Stephen spread among his barons it was the castles of Lord Lovell at Castle Cary and Lord Mowbray at West Harptree which Stephen had to besiege, as well as the castle of the Mohun family at Dunster (Howlett 1886), while in 1139 Hugh de Tracy probably captured the castle of William fitz Odo at Nether Stowey (Renn 1973). It was only while the invaders were more afraid of the English than of one another that they could be relied upon to submit to the discipline imposed by the Conqueror, who oversaw all castle building. Thereafter, the spread of castle building went hand-in-hand with the emergence of feudal politics and the struggle for control of land and vassals, signalled by rebellion and private war. Revolt was often tolerated to the extent that men were not automatically killed for treason and often regained their lands after unsuccessful rebellion.

The castles built by individual barons are important locally in showing the way in which the new disposition of lands after the Norman Conquest led to the aggregation of estates with new central places. Nether Stowey is a good example of a new grouping of lands built up around a castle. Here the lands which had belonged to King Harold were transferred to Alfred of Spain and remained together as a recognisable grouping of estates for some centuries thereafter (Dunning 1981). Dunster formed the centre for the estates of the Mohun family which were mostly grouped in the west of the county and the same is probably true for the lands of the Lovells around their castle at Castle Cary, in the east. These castles formed the caputs of the honours of the new landholders (Aston 1986), at once the chief seat of the family and the centre of their administration. In part, this process was facilitated by royal withdrawal from the county. Many of the old 'central places' passed into the hands of other feudal tenants and probably declined in importance as a result. Thus, Crewkerne was probably granted away by Henry I to Richard de Reviers before 1107, while Martock had passed to Eustace of Boulogne at much the same time (Dunning 1978). Somerset developed no major towns around castles, as for instance occurred at Devizes in Wiltshire (Rowley 1983) and Taunton was the only major town to possess a castle, perhaps begun in 1107 as a hall, with a keep begun in 1138 (Renn 1973).

Unlike some parts of France, the castle did not become the centre of administration in the shire. Instead, quite soon after the Conquest, the new rulers began to use the existing structures which they found in place and, although there was a revolution among the landholders, the government of the shire was continued as before, with the sheriff as the King's representative and the courts as the administrative device through which routine business was carried on. William continued to issue charters and writs and it was through the courts that they were administered.

The hundred, with its court, was the basic unit of local government in late Old English society, but it was perhaps not as old as some people have imagined. No instance of the use of the word occurs in English before the tenth century and so although it is possible that they are older, its seems sensible to consider that the hundreds were introduced during that period (Campbell 1975, p. 46). James Campbell has pointed to the likelihood that the system owed much to late Carolingian governmental methods, but what the English kings of the tenth century did was to adapt the system to their own circumstances. In the south of England, in the long-established shires, the hundreds were clearly modelled to fit the existing political and social geography, so that many hundreds had royal estates as their meeting places (Aston 1985a, p. 35). Of the fifty-eight hundreds in Somerset which were certainly known to exist in the mid-eleventh century (Thorn 1980, pp. 370–1), twenty-three were named from royal estates and others from the estates of major landowners. Despite the term, there is little to suggest that the hundreds ever contained 100 families or 100 hides in Somerset. In 1086, they averaged approximately fifty hides each, but that average conceals widely differing sizes. There is nothing to suggest an underlying regularity – rather it seems that the hundreds were constructed to fit the existing estate groupings, and then frequently altered to suit changing circumstances, particularly the changing ownership of land.

By the mid-eleventh century many hundreds were, in effect, jurisdictions under the supervision, if not the control of the lord of the land. Thus the hundreds of *Tantona* and *Pinpeministra* covered the lands of the later manors and hundred of Taunton and Taunton Deane (Thorn 1980, p. 371). The bishop of Winchester was the effective controller of the hundred and all its revenues (DB 2, 1–4). The hundred of *Licget* probably included only the estate of Coker before the Domesday Book (Thorn 1980, p. 380, n. 80) and this may have been because Coker, the modern East and West Coker, had belonged in 1066 to the countess Gytha, King Harold's queen, and had been withdrawn from the larger Houndsborough hundred. This would have meant that the Countess's men would not have been subject to any other jurisdiction but her own. An administrative adjustment such as this suggests that the hundred was an extremely flexible unit and that changes often took place, so that even if there had been a regular pattern when they were first set up, by the mid-eleventh century this had disappeared.

Some hundreds still carried in their names the implication that the court of the hundred was a public, not a private jurisdiction, as it threatened to become. Many hundred meeting places were at open-air sites, perhaps chosen because they were accessible to all and neutral, rather than being in or close to the king's hall. Thus the two Glastonbury-owned hundreds of *Locheslega* and *Ringandesuuel* (Loxley and Ringwoldeswey), which were later joined to make the hundred of Whitley, both took their names from landscape features rather than estate centres, the first from a lane, now Reynald's Way, in Butleigh (Anderson 1939, p. 51), and the second from a wood, now Loxley Wood, in Shapwick. Both these meeting places were on the ridge of the Poldens and close to the road of Roman origin which runs from east to west. Bempstone Hundred, which covered all of the Wedmore island, was named from its meeting place, which was a stone on the boundary between Chapel Allerton and Weare. Its name meant 'trumpeter's stone' (Anderson 1939, pp. 49–50).

The hundred courts provided local justice, and the sites of their gallows or other places of execution, which are sometimes known, are a reminder that the world of the tenth and eleventh centuries was often violent. At Ashcott, the site of the gallows of Whitley Hundred stands on the ridge on the boundary between Ashcott and Shapwick in a field still called Furches (Lat. *furcas*, a gallows), while other places of execution, are known by the field-name 'hedgestock' from the OE **heafod** + **stoc**, literally 'headpost', the place where the heads of criminals were displayed. Such names exist at Batcombe, Hornblotton, North Cadbury and at Dowlish Wake, near Ilminster. From the standpoint of the king, however, the most important function of the hundred court was as a meeting place between local people and royal officials who collected taxes. In the tenth and eleventh centuries the king's special officer in the shire, replacing the ealdorman as a channel of communication as the latter grew more important was the *scir-gerefa*, the sheriff. He supervised the king's business on the royal estates as well as dealing with taxation. He was paid by the granting of estates and in 1066 the then sheriff, Tovi, had held Lopen, Bradon, Buckland St Mary, Discove, Belluton, Freshford and Berkley (DB).

The shire also had a court which met only twice a year and probably dealt with only the most important business. In 994, the shire court, which included both bishops and ealdormen, annulled a charter which the tenants of land held by Muchelney had gained as the result of misrepresentation. They had converted their three life lease into hereditary tenure thus depriving the monks (Bates 1899, p. 44). Such property disputes were probably among the most important business the court could deal with. The existence of the shire court is, of course, a clear sign of the existence of the shire itself. The kingdom of Mercia had not been 'shired' until the tenth century, but we have seen that some idea of 'Somerset' had probably existed since the early eighth century at the latest and the present historic borders since the fall of Mercia to the Danes.

The system of courts was a manifestation at a local level of a governmental system which depended upon written records and systematic administration (Campbell 1975, p. 46). It was because such a system existed that it was possible to make the Domesday Book through which so much information about Somerset is revealed.

The biggest impact upon the shire undoubtedly came from the revolution in landholding which had taken place in the twenty years between the Conquest and the Domesday Book. Of course, the large secular landholders had changed, as was to be expected, but the same was true of the lesser landowners and English tenants. Of the 622 settlements in Domesday Somerset, which are recorded (Darby 1986, p. 336), 295 or 47·5 per cent were of one hide only or less. Only eleven of these places had the same tenant in 1086 as they had in 1066. For example, Brictric and Wulfward had held Buckland St Mary in 1066 and were now tenants of the king himself (DB 47, 1). Alfward and his brothers held Stocklinch and their father had the property before them in 1066. They now held from the king (DB 47, 14). Even allowing for the natural turnover caused by death, it is clear that the small landowners had suffered grievously. Those men who are only recorded as 'thegns', the holders for the most part of very small estates often as a member of a group, did most badly of all. All were swept away. There was also a tendency for the very small holdings to be amalgamated. Probably estates which were hardly distinguishable as separate agricultural units were being put back together again. Thus Donyatt, three separate units in 1066, belonging to Adolf, Saewin and Dunstan had been joined together to make a single manor for Drogo, the tenant of the Count of Mortain (DB 19, 24). In almost every manor the tenant in 1086 had a Norman-French name.

It is likely that the estates of the major secular landholders were concentrated in fewer hands in 1086 than they had been in 1066. The layman, Alfred of Spain, held just over 37 hides of land, mostly in the Cannington area, which was made up of 25 separate properties, 16 of which had belonged to Alfwy, Banna's son, in 1066. Walter of Douai had 37 manors, totalling 96 hides, and the Count of Mortain had 86 manors in the county. There were only twenty-eight major laymen who held estates directly from the king as tenants-in-chief. Although there are many sub-tenants in the Domesday Book in 1086, there were fewer of them than there had been before the Conquest. By 1086 60 per cent of all land in the county was controlled directly by the landlord. Land granted to sub-tenants was a minor proportion of the total.

The area where change was least obvious was on the estates of the king and the church. The king's estates had always been large. In 1066 they averaged 72 ploughlands each. The estates of the church were also in large holdings. Indeed, the average size of the holdings of king and church was 23·36 ploughlands each.[1] King and church between them held 63 per cent of the county,[2] so that they dominated the countryside, both as prodigious landholders and because they held the largest estates (Fig. 7.2).

Although there had been a revolution in landholding over the course of King William's reign, at the everyday level of rural routine there is little to suggest that the Normans influenced the lives of the peasants much at all. They had inherited a highly structured hierarchy of status and economic power and simply inserted themselves into the superior positions, exploiting the labour of the peasantry as their predecessors had done. The

---

[1] I have used 'ploughlands' and not hides as a measure here because so much of the king's land was not hidated.

[2] In order to calculate this figure I have assumed that the king's 457 ploughlands correspond to two-thirds that number of taxable hides.

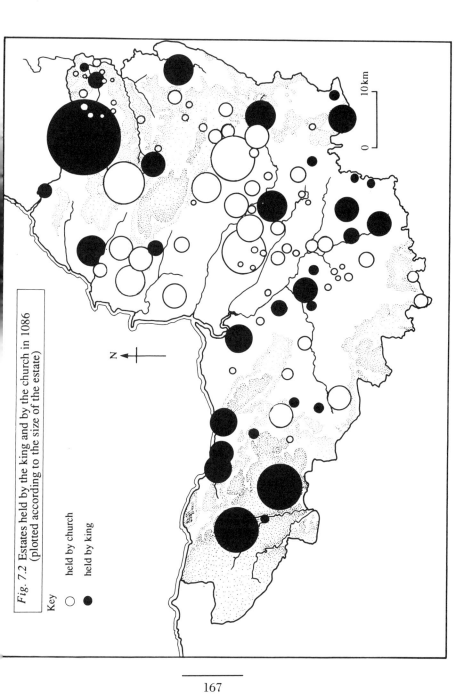

Fig. 7.2 Estates held by the king and by the church in 1086 (plotted according to the size of the estate)

Key

○   held by church

●   held by king

10 km

N

servi, *villani*, *bordarii*, *cotarii* and *coliberti* of the Domesday Book were all part of the social gradations the Normans inherited. However, the imposition of a more thoroughly militarised landholding class than had existed before, together with the heavy demands in taxation made by the new foreign administration placed increased burdens on the peasantry, who were, in the end, the people who paid for everything. As well as finding the money for heavy gelds during the Conqueror's reign, most estates also showed an increase in value. Part of this probably came from heavier stocking with animals and the purchase of more oxen for ploughteams, but since the demesnes were worked chiefly by labour services this implied greater activity on the part of tenants, with services extended. The greatest increases in value probably occurred on lay estates. William de Mohun's estates averaged 17·87 shillings per hide in value in 1066. By 1086 the value was up to 23·6 shillings, a 32 per cent increase. Church estates saw smaller rises in values but they were still significant. At Wells the estates rose in value by 28 per cent; at Glastonbury by 26·9 per cent and at Bath Abbey by 10·12 per cent. An increase in real incomes was thus available for the ruling class in Somerset during the first twenty years of Norman rule. Since Somerset was so much dominated by the church, the bulk of the transfer of value was probably invested in church building, vestments, plate and decoration in churches and in increased manpower, rather than being spent elsewhere. For the laymen, however, a proportion of the extra funds were undoubtedly spent abroad. William the Conqueror spent much of his time campaigning in Normandy and surrounding districts and the reigns of his sons were marked by relentless and almost unceasing warfare in Europe. England, which had supported so much in the way of Danegeld, could evidently support these exactions also.

Since there are so few early surveys surviving from the eleventh century it is very difficult to gauge the extent to which individual estates changed. At Shapwick, the Abbot of Glastonbury had four ploughteams on his demesne in 1086 (DB 8, 5) and in the time of Henry I there were still four teams. However, the 100 sheep on the demesne had been increased to 400, exploiting the moors in the summer and the manorial and estate fallow in winter (R.5.33, fo. 115).[3] Early in the twelfth century, during the reign of Henry I, many of the Abbey of Glastonbury's manors were let to rent and returned varying sums to the abbey, often less than the value noted in 1086. Thus, at Brent, the estate which had been valued at £50 in 1086 was worth £40 in rent in the early years of the twelfth century, although this had risen to £80 by 1171. Wrington, valued at £30 in 1086, had fallen back to £20 and then risen by 1171 to £25. High Ham had remained solidly worth £10 from 1086 to 1171. Very few estates were worth more in the time of Henry I than in 1086 or even in 1201, when the first full survey becomes available. The manpower on the manors then seems to have been no greater, indeed often less, than the manpower in 1086 (R.5.33, ff. 110v–114). Demesnes were of much the size that they had been in 1086 and the stocking with ploughteams and other animals seems to have been comparable. Glastonbury, at least, had not increased its income, indeed it had probably lost by the growth of small scutage tenants, who paid only small fixed rents.

It must be to the estates of lay owners that we should turn for growth in population and the extension of agriculture. Unfortunately documentary evidence is very sparse. As we have seen there is every reason to believe that the pattern of settlement had been established by the early eleventh century and the countryside filled with settlements. Any expansion must have come through the growth of the open-fields of individual settlements and the intensification of cultivation in those areas where that was possible. At East Pennard, the number of holdings in 1189 was exactly double the number of villein holdings which had existed in 1086. They had been created by dividing each villein holding in two, creating half-virgates (pers. comment, Mrs Penny Stokes). It is likely that on other estates new holdings were created by extending the common fields into areas of pasture or waste, thus reducing the stock capacity of the manor in favour of arable. The very common field-name 'breach' occurs in many parishes in Somerset and its position, within the open-

---

[3] The details below about the value of the Glastonbury estates come from manuscript R.5.33. This contains, inter alia, an inquisition of *c.* 1171 of Hilbert the Precentor, which compares values for the time of Henry I with 1171.

fields, suggests the break-up of previously uncultivated ground for new arable. The name was certainly in use in Somerset by the thirteenth century. The purpose of the division of holdings was probably to increase the rent-paying capacity of the manor and also to provide more labour services to work the demesne. It is unlikely that they were created in response to demographic pressure, since it is unlikely that peasant families could be formed if there were no holdings for young men to take up. Instead, the creation of holdings would have allowed the formation of new families as hitherto celibate and unmarried younger sons left their father's holdings to work the new farms. Smaller properties always carry a higher rent per acre than large ones and the new labour services would have represented a real increase in income to the abbey.

The growth of towns also implies increased economic activity and there is good evidence for this in the century after the Conquest. All the towns of the Old English period continued to flourish, while new towns were begun by Norman lords who wished to exploit the financial advantages of town ownership, while adopting the practice familiar to them in Normandy. The Borough of Montacute had already been founded, alongside the castle, before the foundation of the priory, and was granted to the new monastery in 1102 (SRS 8 1894). It has been suggested that the town is now represented by the street named 'Bishopston' in Montacute, with the present 'Borough', representing a foundation of the thirteenth century (Aston and Leech 1977, p. 105). Downend may have existed by the middle of the century (Aston and Leech 1977, p. 39) and Dunster may have been established by the early twelfth century. The borough of Nether Stowey probably began as an adjunct to the castle in the same way, quite soon after the castle was built (Dunning 1981).

Lordship and the desire to profit from a new town also explains why towns grew up at Glastonbury and at Wells. Glastonbury was certainly in existence by the end of the twelfth century and was a small planned town, built to serve the abbey (Aston and Leech 1977, p. 57). Wells seems to have been developed as a borough in the mid-twelfth century, when the bishop returned from Bath (Aston and Leech 1977, p. 147). The modern plan of the town reveals that it was laid out with respect to the old Anglo-Saxon Minster, before the new Cathedral, with its more accurate east-west alignment, was built. These towns were part of a general movement whereby the interest of the crown declined and that of local landholders grew as economic activity increased and market towns and fairs were founded by church and landowners. Consequently, siting of such towns and markets often depended on the interests and property of their founders, rather than obeying rational rules relating to catchment areas. Nevertheless, the success of many of them, at least through the Middle Ages, testifies to the suitability of many sites and to the commercial acumen of their founders (Gerrard 1987, p. 110).

The effect of the Conquest was to concentrate lands into fewer hands and, since so much land was held in return for military service, on the surface it should have been more difficult for land to change hands. In fact, although the Normans introduced a system which made testamentary disposition of property more difficult than it had been for the English and placed more emphasis on primogeniture (Holt 1982), there is some evidence which points to the dispersal of land among many lesser families. Partly this was because once land had been granted as feudal tenancies, in the years after the Conquest, it tended to remain in one family and very quickly attained hereditable status. In this way much land which had been closely tied to monasteries in the mid-eleventh century passed to vassals and escaped from monastic control. Thus Shepton Mallet, which was part of the Glastonbury estate of Pilton in 1086 (DB 5, 20), was held by Roger of Courseulles as a fee, by military tenure at that date. By the end of the twelfth century it was in the hands of William Malet, who held a total of twelve knights' fees there and on the Poldens (R.5.33, fo. 117r) while Lamyatt, near Bruton, which was granted to Nigel, William the Conqueror's doctor, to hold from the abbey, also became separated from Glastonbury. By the end of the twelfth century it was in the hands of Philip de Columbaris who held it along with Woolavington as a single knight's fee. The village was to stay in the hands of his family for several generations. In addition to the major military tenants, the abbey also had many lesser tenants who were described in 1197 as holding 'per scutagium', that is as military tenants, but with too little land to be considered as knight's fees. Thomas Spirewyt held a hide at Pylle in Brent and Robert Malherbe held half a hide in Wrington (R.5.33, fo. 117v). These men, with their French Christian names and toponymic surnames, were the descendants of the Norman settlers. A similar process occurred with the lands of laymen. They were no more able to deprive their military tenants of their estates than the church could, so that lesser vassals also came to be the effective owners of land granted on military tenures to their fathers and grandfathers. Thus both on church and on lay estates, what had started as the grant of land in return for military service had become permanent alienation. Landholding for the descendants of the Conqueror's soldiers had become very secure. Although it is difficult to know much about the landmarket in the first century after the Conquest, it is clear that, by the time the first deeds begin to appear, many small estates existed. Their owners often held fractions of a knight's fee and owed suit at a manorial court. They were in effect minor freeholders, only minimally dependent on the lord of the estate and free to sell their land and move if they wished. Ownership of the soil and lordship were effectively becoming divorced, allowing for increased social mobility and diversity as the 'free' men of society multiplied.

Church and foreigners

Despite the way in which the church had burgeoned in the tenth century, ecclesiastical practice in England in the mid-eleventh century was very provincial and backward. The incumbent Archbishop of Canterbury, Stigand, was closely associated with Harold's regime, and was not trusted by King William. By 1070 he had been removed and replaced with Lanfranc, one of William's most trusted clerics and a man of probity and intelligence. He was in sharp contrast to his predecessor, who had obtained his office while there was still an existing Archbishop of Canterbury, held the see of Winchester in plurality and had obtained his pallium from Pope Benedict X in 1058, an intruder into the Papacy (Barlow 1979, p. 78). With Lanfranc and with the Normans came the Gregorian reforms, so that the church in Somerset was affected doubly, by its invasion and colonisation by foreigners, who took over the church as a source of power and/or wealth, just as they took over the land, and by the introduction of new ways of relating the religious to the secular worlds.

We have already seen that the Abbey of Glastonbury lost its English abbot to the Normans. On his death he was replaced by a monk from Caen, Thurstan, who ruled from 1077/8 to 1096, although his abbacy was marked by scandal when his quarrel with the monks culminated in the shooting dead of three of them in the abbey church and the wounding of eighteen more by soldiers in the abbot's employ (ASC 1083). The cause of the quarrel was the desire of the new abbot to introduce the chant used at Caen into the Abbey. Although Thurstan was sent back to Normandy he did not lose office and returned to England under William Rufus, while the English monks, who had rebelled were sent to other houses (Knowles 1963, pp. 114–15). These events were probably symptomatic of the feeling and attitudes in other Somerset monasteries as new continental practice was introduced by foreign abbots. Successive abbots after Thurstan also came from Normandy and, in 1126, Henry of Blois, the nephew of Henry I and grandson of the Conqueror, became abbot at Glastonbury. This association had its advantages, since it made defence of the abbey's rights easier, and made possible the reacquisition of lost lands (Scott 1981, p. 161). Muchelney and Athelney seem to have been in a state of dependence upon Glastonbury, thus making it easier to control them (Scott 1981, p. 155). At Bath, however, the pre-Conquest English Abbot, Elsig, continued to rule until his death in 1087. As the ruling class in Somerset became Norman, so the monks of the monasteries were drawn from the same group and the lower ranks were also normanised. The habit of appointing abbots from Normandy and other parts of France continued under Rufus and Henry I (Knowles 1963, p. 112).

From the years just after the Conquest, foreign monasteries were granted lands in Somerset. St Stephen's monastery at Caen, William the Conqueror's foundation, was given the church at Crewkerne, together with its ten hides (DB 12, 1) and St Mary's Abbey at Montebourg had an estate in the Frome area (DB 13, 1), but the Conquest was far more important in that it opened up England to new foundations as the new monastic orders spread across Europe. Somerset was in some ways a difficult county in which to found a new monastery, since it was already heavily provided with existing houses. The Cluniac priory of Montacute, was founded c. 1100 by William Count of Mortain, who gave the new monastery the borough of Montacute, the castle and the demesne of the manor of Bishopston and other properties (Dunning 1974, p. 213). Other monastic houses of the period before 1154 include the Augustinian canons of Bruton, founded in 1142 by William de Mohun, who endowed the monastery with the manor and churches of Bruton (SRS 8 1894); the Augustinian canons of Taunton, perhaps founded around 1115, by the Bishop of Winchester (Page 1911, p. 141) and the Priory of Benedictine nuns at Cannington, founded *c.* 1138 (Page 1911, p. 109). In each case, these houses, Taunton excepted, along with the later Keynsham Abbey, were founded in centres which had formerly been royal estates and had passed into the hands of great vassals of the crown. The new houses provided for the growing numbers of men and women of good birth in the countryside who wished to enter the religious life. As a group, these new houses made little impact on the county as landowners. They were a visible expression of the power of the regular life within twelfth-century society, which was to continue with the foundation of the Cistercian house at Cleeve and the two Carthusian monasteries of Witham and Hinton. While the ancient Benedictine foundations continued as examples of the continuity of existence and the adaptation of the local to new forms, the newer foundations were mostly affected by the new forms of organisation which made orders such as the Cluniacs or the Cistercians so powerful throughout western Europe. Through them, the spirit of the imperial and universal church of the twelfth century was introduced into Somerset. It was inevitable that it should be effected through the colonisation of the English church.

The changes which took place inside the secular church were no less important. Bishop Giso, who ruled at Wells from 1060 until 1088, had reformed the cathedral by imposing the rule of St Chrodegang on the chapter (Page 1911, p. 8). He came from Flanders and his successor John de Villula was a Norman. His first act was to move his seat to Bath. This was the result of a desire to be canonically correct in siting a bishop's seat in a town rather than at a rural centre and fitted the pattern familiar to the Norman prelates from their homeland. However, the early bishops and their followers were not yet deeply imbued with the spirit of reform. The new bishop's brother became the steward at Wells and many of the demesne church lands were engrossed by him and passed on to his son John, who was Archdeacon of Wells. He, in turn, left the lands to his brother Reginald, who was the Precentor. In the mid-twelfth century, the lands had to be repurchased from Reginald's nephews by the bishop (Page 1911, pp. 11–12). This was an excellent example of the sort of abuse which the Gregorian reforms set out to stop – in this case aggravated by the way in which a group of foreign relatives of the bishop had carved up the diocesan lands for their family advantage.

The organisation of the church in Somerset in the century or two after the Conquest, as before it, is hardly understood. The English were rather late and unsystematic in the employment of the archdeacon as the principal administrative officer of the bishop (Barlow 1979, p. 247). This may have been because, in many places, some vestiges of the old collegiate system of extended parishes still existed, as for instance at Crewkerne, so that direct contact with the bishop was easy. It may also have been because so many priests were, effectively, the men of the lay lord who owned the church in which they served. However, as the priest came to be seen as a member of an independent order, not beholden to the laity for his authority, and as the sheer numbers of clergy grew, so an organisation which could discipline the clergy was needed. There was certainly an archdeacon in Somerset by 1086, since Benzelin the Archdeacon held Congresbury church at that date from the bishop (DB 6, 14). His name suggests that he was not English. During the next century other archdeacons appeared, so that by the mid-twelfth century the machinery of government was in place (D & C, Wells, I, p. 39).

The building and foundation of churches continued after the Norman conquest as before, and some 150 surviving Norman fonts, as well as fragments of masonry in existing churches, testify to the vigour with which this expansion continued (Bettey 1988, p. 56). The fonts are specially important since they were a sign of the independent status of their church. The existence of churches in the century after the Conquest is often revealed incidentally, and in some cases the churches were in existence so soon after 1086 that it is difficult to avoid the conclusion that some of them predate the conquest. Thus, at Montacute Priory, the foundation charter, granted *c.* 1102, includes the gift of the churches of Tintinhull, Creech St Michael, East Chinnock, 'Hunesberg', Closworth, Mudford, Yarlington, Brympton and Odcombe (SRS 8 1894). At Old Cleeve, the church was given to the Abbey of Bec-Hellouin by the very early twelfth century, while the church at Halse was granted to the Knights of St John of Jerusalem in 1159 (Dunning 1985, pp. 37, 79). These were all very ordinary settlements and some were very small. It seems unlikely that these places alone had churches. On the contrary, probably a majority of settlements had a church of their own by 1100. This movement was fuelled by the continuing growth of independent estates. New lords began to treat their new lands as their private property, and the evidence usually appears when, impelled by the new morality about the ownership of churches by laymen, they gave the churches to a monastery or to the cathedral. Thus the individualism of the Norman lords of Somerset completed what their English predecessors had begun, while the new centralised administration of the bishop gradually undermined the jurisdiction of the old minster churches.

Conclusions

It is much easier to start a history than it is to stop. We started with chaos, the supposedly unformed landscape and we finish with Somerset. But the first farmers we know about, in the Neolithic period, were by no means the first people here and we know little of the social process which brought them into Somerset and set them off on their path as farmers. Their descendants were the men and women of the Bronze Age and then the men and women of the Iron Age, of the Roman period, the Old Welsh period and finally the English period. Although there were incomers who brought with them new ways of organising society and new languages, there is no evidence to suggest that the old people were driven out or destroyed. Only the social upheaval of the modern period, with its access to new transport has substantially changed the people of the countryside.

Nevertheless it is possible to pick out several important themes in the making of Somerset. The first of these hardly needs to be stated, that the landscape of Somerset has been evolving under the pressure of agriculture since the beginning of the Neolithic era and that there has been no time since then when Somerset has been a 'wilderness'. We live in a ancient landscape, shaped almost completely by men.

The second theme was signalled by the appearance of hillforts. They marked the establishment of an organised, hierarchical society, probably dominated by warriors. It also marks the appearance of overt territoriality and clearly has to do with the control of scarce resources. It was the development of one particular hillfort, at South Cadbury, that determined the political geography of central Somerset, as long as it existed in a state of tension with the region to the east.

When the tension was relieved as the result of incorporation into a single state, whether Roman or English, the emphasis moved to the newly created site at Ilchester which provided a political focus for the aristocracy, replacing the hillfort. The town retained its importance as a trade centre into the Middle Ages. By 1276 it contained twelve parishes and by 1166 had become the site of a county gaol and was the site of the shire court and later circuit courts (Dunning 1974, pp. 185–7). Ilchester became important in the Roman period because the surrounding area was suitable for exploitation by intensive farming. The new authorities made use of the structure of native society to construct their own political system, using the newly built road system, which linked the eastern side of Somerset from north to south and taking advantage of the town's position between the trade routes from the east and the marshes and the roads to the sea on the west.

If the heart of the later county was to grow from the interplay between geography and the structure of the aristocracy, the countryside grew from the control of scarce resources by the same group. As a group, they were more vulnerable than the peasantry, since, as the rulers of the countryside, they were the people most likely to be dispossessed in the event of war. Yet the landscape which they ruled shows a series of changes which follow naturally from what went before. Culturally, the invaders, whether they were English or Normans were too like the men they superseded for a line of development to be broken. We know so little about the organisation of the landscape before the post-Roman period that we cannot know if the existence of the multiple estate can be carried back past the fifth or sixth century AD, but thereafter it is the base upon which subsequent change was founded. This way of organising the land provided a basis for the primitive aristocracy grouped around its leader, the king, who was himself primarily a great landlord and a warrior, the leader of a kin-group and probably related to those around him. Such a leader monopolised communications and contact with other groups, particularly trading and diplomatic contacts, and maintained his position partly by gift relationship with his followers. For the king in his rural hall, the central places on his estates provided a natural focus for his activities. It is likely that his major followers structured their own relationships in much the same way. Such a world was rigidly ordered and probably based upon kin-groups at all levels, with the idea of lordship and the patronage which sprang from it, providing the social glue that held it all together.

The break-up of the 'multiple estate' was a major economic and social event. Spurred on by the need to reward followers and then to raise troops, the Anglo-Saxon kings of Wessex encouraged the creation of a new pattern of landholding that profoundly affected the way the countryside was organised. As private property appeared, a new 'class' was created, who extended the warrior elite both in numbers and in hierarchy, so that the idea of the thegn suffered considerable change. That pressure of change was probably behind the 'Compilation on Status', and shows a society beginning to be self-conscious enough to define roles in terms of an ideal, which was probably already outdated when it was formulated.

Although it would be easy to see the tenth century as a time of disorder, the reality was that it was a more peaceful time than the preceding centuries and the combination of a reorganised landscape and a more peaceful world led to a rise in population and a real increase in wealth. Towns were necessary to cope with the increased travel and trade and they grew once more out of the need of kings to exploit their society, this time to increase their wealth, rather than their soldiers. Towns were not, therefore, a natural and unplanned addition to the structure of tenth-century Somerset; they were the result of a policy and their aim was political, in that the king thereby retained control of an important sector of the growing economy for his own benefit.

Town and country were shaped for the purposes of the king

and the ruling group who surrounded and supported him, and it was their decisions which determined the existence of villages and fields, towns and woods. At no times is it possible to see the peasants as important in the shaping of their world; they were the agents who cultivated the land and paid the geld. In a world which was so much a customary society, in which the majority bowed to the ends of the minority with little if any open coercion, the cement which held everything together was the power of religion. This was a common bond between peasant and lord, something which was as true of the Roman world as it was of the Celtic or the English. I have dealt with religion as if it were a separate and discrete area of life. The reality was that it so permeated ancient and medieval society that no part of life was free from its influence. At all times it provided an explanation for the existence of man and his world and it also provided a means of propitiating the natural powers of the world. For the men of Roman Somerset the adaptation and assimilation of their native gods to the gods of the Roman world at once symbolised their inclusion within the Empire. For the Celtic Christians and then for the pagan English, the church brought them within the community of thought and belief which succeeded the Roman Empire and out of which western Europe was born. Literacy and belief went hand in hand.

For the kings of Wessex, the church was an institution which offered them legitimacy and support as they built their kingdom and English Somerset was formed as much by the foundation of minsters as by the take-over of multiple estates. Monasteries were bulwarks against the terrors of a landscape peopled with devils and an unseen world of spiritual forces, and they were also symbols of the power and legitimate authority of kings who had founded them. The later development of the church reflects the changes in English society. The spread of secular churches and the increase in the wealth of revived monasteries followed the reorganisation of the ruling elite. Just as kings had built minsters, so thegns built chapels on their estates as adjuncts of their status, or if they were rich, made donations of land to the monasteries to ensure the aid of the monks in their struggle to enter the next world on favourable terms and, meanwhile, to help their survival in this one. The growth of church organisation reflected the growing sophistication of secular society. Without order and calm, Christianity could not flourish. Where it did, it provided the exemplar for the life of both society and individuals.

The Norman Conquest was a less profound upheaval than its name and reputation suggest. What it did do was to push Somerset society away from its insularity in religious matters, and reduce the role of the king in secular matters. The overwhelming victory of William the Conqueror opened the way to a Somerset in which the power of local lords came to dominate As a result forces were set in motion which were to lead to the break-up of unitary lordship and the destruction of demesne agriculture. As the relationship between the aristocracy and the land changed, slavery and an unfree peasantry were also destined to disappear.

Bibliography

Abels, R. P. (1988) *Lordship and Military Obligation in Anglo-Saxon England*, London.

Alcock, L. (1972) *'By South Cadbury is that Camelot...'* The Excavation of Cadbury Castle, 1966–1970, London.

Alcock, L. (1987) 'Cadbury-Camelot: a fifteen-year perspective', in *Economy, Society and Warfare among the Britons and Saxons*, ed. L. Alcock, Cardiff.

Anderson, O. S. (1939) *The English Hundred Names: The South Western Counties*, Lund.

ApSimon, A. M., Donovan, D. T. & Taylor, H. (1960–61) 'The statigraphy and archaeology of the late-glacial and post-glacial deposits at Brean Down, Somerset', *Proceedings of the University of Bristol Spelaeological Society*, **9**, 67–136.

ApSimon, A. M., Rahtz, P. A. & Harris, L. G. (1958) 'The Iron Age "A" ditch and pottery at Pagans Hill, Chew Stoke', *Proceedings of the University of Bristol Spelaeological Society*, **8**, 97–105.

Archer, S. (1979) 'Late Roman gold and silver hoards in Britain: a gazetteer', in *The End of Roman Britain*, ed. P. J. Casey, BAR, British Series, 71, Oxford.

Aston, M. (1984) 'The towns of Somerset', in *The Anglo-Saxon Towns of Southern England*, ed. J. Haslam, Chichester.

Aston, M. (1985a) *Interpreting the Landscape*, London.

Aston, M. (1985b) 'Rural settlement in Somerset: some preliminary thoughts', in *Medieval Villages*, ed. D. Hooke, OUCA Monograph No. 5, Oxford.

Aston, M. (1986) 'Post-Roman central places in Somerset', in *Central Places, Archaeology and History*, ed. E. Grant, Sheffield.

Aston, M. (ed.) (1988) *Aspects of the Medieval Landscape of Somerset*, Taunton.

Aston, M. (ed.) (1989a) *The Shapwick Project: A Topographical and Historical Survey*, 2nd Report, Bristol.

Aston, M. (1989b) 'The development of medieval rural settlement in Somerset', in *Landscape and Townscape in the South-West*, ed. R. Higham, Exeter Studies in History 22, Exeter.

Aston, M. & Burrow, I. (1982) 'The early Christian centres 600–1000 AD', in *The Archaeology of Somerset: A Review to 1500 AD*, ed. Aston and Burrow, Taunton.

Aston, M. & Iles, R. (1987) *The Archaeology of Avon*, Bristol.

Aston, M. & Leech, R. (1977) *Historic Towns in Somerset*, Bristol.

Aston, M., Austin, D. & Dyer, C. (1989) *The Rural Settlements of Medieval England: Studies Dedicated to Maurice Beresford and John Hurst*, Oxford.

BAFU (Birmingham University Field Archaeology Unit) (1990) *Romans in Shepton Mallet: Excavations at Fosse Lane, 1990*, Birmingham.

Balch, H. E. (1926) 'Chelms Combe Shelter', *PSANHS*, **72**, 97–123.

Balch, H. E. (1928) 'Excavations at Wookey Hole and other Mendip caves, 1926–7', in *Antiquaries Journal*, **8**, 193–210.

Barlow, F. (1979) *The English Church, 1000–1066*, 2nd ed., London.

Barrett, J. C. (1987) 'The Glastonbury Lake Village: models and source criticism', *Archaeological Journal*, **144**, 409–23.

Bates, E. H. (ed.) (1899) *Two Cartularies of the Benedictine Abbeys of Muchelney and Athelney in the County of Somerset*, Somerset Record Society, Vol. 14, Taunton.

Batt, J. (1975) 'The burghal hidage – Axbridge', *PSANHS*, **119**.

Bede (1910) *Bede's Ecclesiastical History of the English Nation*, London.

Biddle, M. (1976) 'Towns', in *The Archaeology of Anglo-Saxon England*, ed. D. M. Wilson, London.

Blair, J. (1985) 'Secular minster churches in Domesday Book', in *Domesday Books: A Reassessment*, ed. P. Sawyer, London.

Blair, J. (1988a) 'Minster churches in the landscape', in *Anglo-Saxon Settlement*, ed. D. Hooke, Oxford.

Blair, J. (ed.) (1988b) *Minster and Parish Churches: The Local Church in Transition*, Oxford.

Bradley, R. (1984) *The Social Foundations of Prehistoric Britain*, London.

Branigan, K. (1972) 'The Romano-British villa at Brislington', *PSANHS*, **116**, 78–85.

Branigan, K. (1977) *Gatcombe Roman Villa*, BAR, British Series, 44, Oxford.

Brooks, N. (1989a) 'The creation and early structure of the kingdom of Kent', in *The Origins of the Anglo-Saxon Kingdoms*, ed. S. Basset, Leicester.

Brooks, N. (1989b) 'The formation of the Mercian kingdom', in *The Origins of the Anglo-Saxon Kindoms*, ed. S. Basset, Leicester.

Bulleid, A. & Gray, H. St G. (1911 & 1917) *The Glastonbury Lake Village*, 1 and 2, Glastonbury.

Bulleid, A. & Horne, Dom. E. (1926) 'The Roman house at Keynsham, Somerset', *Archaeologia*, **25**, 109–38.

Burgess, C. (1974) 'The Bronze Age', in *British Prehistory: A New Outline*, ed. C. Renfrew, London.

Burrow, I. (1981) *Hillfort and Hilltop Settlement in Somerset in the First to Eighth Centuries A.D.*, BAR, British Series, 91, Oxford.

Burrow, I. (1982) 'Hillforts and hilltops 1000 BC–1000 AD', in *The Archaeology of Somerset: A Review to 1500 AD*, ed. Aston and Burrow, Taunton.

Campbell, A. (1962) *The Chronicle of Æthelweard*, London.

Campbell, J. (1975) 'Observations on English government from the tenth to the twelfth century', *TRHS*, **25**, 39–54.

Campbell, J. (1979) 'Bede's words for places', in *Names, Words and Graves: Early Medieval Settlement*, ed. P. H. Sawyer, Leeds.

Campbell, J., John, E. & Wormald, P. (1982) *The Anglo-Saxons*, Oxford.

Carley, J. (ed.) (1978) *John of Glastonbury Cronica*, BAR, British Series, 41, Oxford.

Carley, J. (1988) *Glastonbury Abbey: The Holy House at the Head of the Moors Adventurous*, Woodbridge.

Carley, J. & Abrams, L. (1991) *The Archaeology and History of Glastonbury Abbey*, Woodbridge.

Coles, B. & Coles, J. (1989) *People of the Wetlands: Bogs, Bodies and Lakedwellers*, London.

Coles, J. M. (1978) 'Man and the landscape in the Somerset Levels', in *The Effects of Man on the Landscape*, ed. S. Limbury and J. Evans, CBA Research Report, 21, London.

Coles, J. (1982) 'Prehistory in the Somerset Levels 4000–100 BC', in *The Archaeology of Somerset: A Review to 1500 AD*, ed. Aston and Burrow, Taunton.

Coles, J. M. (1987) *Meare Village East: The Excavations of A. Bulleid and H. St George Gray 1932–1956*, Exeter.

Coles, J. M. (1989) 'Prehistoric settlement in the Somerset Levels', in *Somerset Levels Papers, 15*, ed. J. M. Coles, Exeter.

Coles, J. & Orme, B. (1984) 'Archaeology in the Somerset Levels 1983', in *Somerset Levels Papers, 10*, ed. J. Coles, B. Orme and S. Rouillard, Cambridge.

Collingwood, R. G. & Wright, R. P. (1965) *The Roman Inscriptions of Britain. I Inscriptions on Stone*, Oxford.

Collinson, J. (1791) *History and Antiquities of the County of Somerset*, 3 vols, Bath.

Corcos, N. J. (1984) 'Early estates on the Poldens and the origins of settlement at Shapwick', *PSANHS*, **127**, 47–54.

Costen, M. D. (1983) 'Stantonbury and district in the tenth century', *Bristol and Avon Archaeology*, **II**, 25–34.

Costen, M. D. (1985) 'Rimpton in Somerset – a late Saxon Estate', *Southern History*, **7**, 13–24.

Costen, M. D. (1989) 'A survey of the Manor of Shapwick in 1327 from the Egerton Manuscript 3321 in the British Library', in *The Shapwick Project: A Topographical and Historical Survey*, ed. M. A. Aston, 2nd Report, Bristol.

Costen, M. D. (1991a) 'Dunstan, Glastonbury and the economy of Somerset in the tenth century', in N. L. Ramsey, M. Sparks and T. Tatton-Brown, forthcoming.

Costen, M. D. (1991b) 'Some evidence for new settlements and field systems in late Anglo-Saxon Somerset', in *The Archaeology and History of Glastonbury Abbey*, ed. J. Carley and L. Abrams, Woodbridge.

Costen, M. D. (1992) 'Huish and Worth: Old English survivals in a later landscape', *Landscape History*, forthcoming.

Costen, M. D. (1988) 'The late Saxon landscape: the evidence from charters and place-names', in *Aspects of the Medieval Landscape of Somerset*, ed. M. Aston, Taunton.

Cunliffe, B. (1974) *Iron Age Communities in Britain*, London.

Cunliffe, B. (1982) 'Iron Age settlements and pottery 650 BC–60 AD', in *The Archaeology of Somerset: A Review to 1500 AD*, ed. Aston and Burrow, Taunton.

Cunliffe, B. (1984a) 'Saxon Bath', in *The Anglo-Saxon Towns of Southern England*, ed. J. Haslam, Chichester.

Cunliffe, B. (1984b) *Danebury: An Iron Age Hillfort in Hampshire 1 & 2: The Excavations 1969–78*, London.

Cunliffe, B. (1985) *The Temple of Sulis Minerva at Bath. Vol. 1: The Site*, Oxford.

Cunliffe, B. (1986) *The City of Bath*, Gloucester.

Darby, H. C. (1977) *Domesday England*, Cambridge.

Darby, H. C. (1986) *Domesday England*, Cambridge.

Darby, H. C. & Welldon Finn, R. (eds) (1967) *The Domesday Geography of South-Western England*, Cambridge.

Darvill, T. (1987a) 'Neolithic Avon', in *The Archaeology of Avon*, ed. Aston and Iles, Bristol.

Darvill, T. (1987b) *Prehistoric Britain*, London.

Davison, B. K. (1972) 'Castle Neroche: an abandoned Norman fortress in south Somerset', *PSANHS*, **116**, 16–58.

Dickinson, H. (ed.) (1889) 'Nomina Villarum for Somerset of 16 Edward III', in *Kirby's Quest for Somerset*, Somerset Record Society, Vol. 3, Taunton.

Dumville, D. N. (1977a) 'Sub-Roman Britain: history and legend', *History*, **62**, 173–92.

Dumville, D. N. (1977b) 'Kingship, genealogies and the regnal lists', in *Early Medieval Kingship*, ed. P. H. Sawyer and I. N. Woods, Leeds.

Dunning, R. W. (ed.) (1974) *A History of the County of Somerset*, Vol. III, London.

Dunning, R. W. (ed.) (1978) *A History of the County of Somerset*, Vol. IV, London.

Bibliography

Dunning, R. W. (1981) 'The Origins of Nether Stowey', *PSANHS*, **125**, 124–6.

Dunning, R. W. (ed.) (1985) *A History of the County of Somerset*, Vol. V, Oxford.

Dymond, D. (1902) *Worlebury, an Ancient Stronghold in the County of Somerset*, Bristol.

Edwards, H. (1986) 'Two documents from Aldhelm's Malmesbury', *Bulletin of the Institute of Historical Research*, **59**, 139, 1–19.

Edwards, H. (1988) *The Charters of the Early West Saxon Kingdom*, BAR, British Series, 198, Oxford.

Ekwall, E. (1960) *The Concise Oxford Dictionary of English Place-Names*, 4th ed., Oxford.

Ekwall, E. (1964) 'Old English "wic" place-names', *Nomina Germanica*, **13**, Lund.

Elkington, H. D. H. (1976) 'The Mendip lead industry', in *The Roman West Country*, ed. K. Branigan and P. J. Fowler, Newton Abbot.

Ellison, A. (1981) 'Towards a socioeconomic model for the Middle Bronze Age in southern England', in *Pattern of the Past: Studies in Honour of David Clarke*, ed. I. Hodder, G. Isaac and N. Hammond, Cambridge.

Ellison, A. (1982) 'Bronze Age societies 2000–650 BC', in *The Archaeology of Somerset: A Review to 1500 AD*, ed. Aston and Burrow, Taunton.

Esmonde Cleary, A. S. (1989) *The Ending of Roman Britain*, London.

Finberg, H. P. R. (1964) *The Early Charters of Wessex*, Leicester.

Finberg, H. P. R. (1974) *The Formation of England 550–1042*, London.

Fleming R. (1985) 'Monastic lands and England's defence in the Viking age', *EHR*, **100**, 247–65.

Foster, S. (1987) 'A gazetteer of the Anglo-Saxon sculpture in historic Somerset', *PSANHS*, **131**, 49–80.

Fowler, P. (ed.) (1968) *Archaeological Review, No. 3*, Bristol.

Fowler, P. (ed.) (1969) *Archaeological Review, No. 4*, Bristol.

Fowler, P. (ed.) (1970) *Archaeological Review, No. 5*, Bristol.

Fowler, P. (1978) 'Pre-medieval fields in the Bristol region', in *Early Land Allotment in the British Isles: A Survey of Recent Work*, ed. H. C. Bowen and P. J. Fowler, BAR, British Series, 48, Oxford.

Fowler, P. & Rahtz, P. (1972) 'Somerset A.D. 400–700', in *Archaeology and Landscape*, ed. P. Fowler, London.

Fox, E. & Fox, C. (1958) 'Wansdyke reconsidered', *Archaeological Journal*, **115**, 1–45.

Fox, H. S. A. (1981) 'Approaches to the adoption of the Midland System', in *The Origins of Open-Field Agriculture*, ed. T. Rowley, London.

Frend, W. H. C. (1982) 'Romano-British Christianity and the West: comparison and contrast', in *The Early Church in Western Britain and Ireland*, ed. S. M. Pearce, BAR, British Series, 102, Oxford.

Frere, S. (1987) *Britannia*, 3rd ed., London.

Gelling, M. (1967) 'English place-names derived from the compound wicham', *Medieval Archaeology*, **XI**, 87–104.

Gerrard, C. (1987) 'Trade and settlement in medieval Somerset', unpublished Ph.D. thesis, University of Bristol.

Gillingham, J. (1989) '"The most precious jewel in the English crown": levels of danegeld and heregeld in the early eleventh century', *EHR*, **124**, 373–83.

Green, J. P. (1975) 'Bath and other small western towns', in *Small Towns of Roman Britain*, ed. W. Rodwell and T. Rowley, BAR, British Series, 15, Oxford.

Green, M. J. (1976) *The Religions of Civilian Roman Britain*, BAR, British Series, 24, Oxford.

Gregson, N. (1985) 'The multiple estate model: some critical questions', *Journal of Historical Geography*, **11**, 339–51.

Grinsell, L. V. (1970) *The Archaeology of Exmoor*, Newton Abbot.

Grinsell, L. V. (1971) 'Somerset barrows, part II: north and east', supplement to *PSANHS*, **115**, Taunton.

Grinsell, L. V. (1973) *Bath Mint*, Bath.

Haddan, A. W. & Stubbs, W. (1871) *Councils and Ecclesiastical Documents relating to Great Britain and Ireland, Vol. 3*, Oxford.

Hall, D. N. (1985) 'Late Saxon topography and early medieval estates', in *Medieval Villages*, ed. D. Hooke, OUCA Monograph No. 5, Oxford.

Hamilton, N. E. S. A. (ed.) (1870) *William of Malmesbury, De Gestis Pontificum Anglorum*, Roll Series, 52, London.

Haselgrove, C. (1987) *Iron Age Coinage in South-East England*, BAR, British Series, 174, Oxford.

Hassall, J. M. & Hill, D. (1970) 'Pont de l'Arche: Frankish influence on the West Saxon burh?', *Archaeological Journal*, **127**.

Haverfield, F. J. (1906) 'Romano-British Somerset', in *A History of the County of Somerset, Vol. 1*, ed. W. Page, London.

Henderson, J. (1987) 'The Iron Age of Loughey and Meare: some inferences from glass analysis', *Antiquaries Journal*, **68**, 29–42.

Herlihy, D. (1985) *Medieval Households*, London.

Herren, M. W. (1990) 'Gildas and early British monasticism', in *Britain 400–600: Language and History*, ed. A. Bammesberger and A. Wollmann, Heidelberg.

Hibbert, F. A. (1978) 'Vegetational history of the Somerset Levels', in *The Effects of Man on the Landscape*, ed. S. Limbury and J. Evans, CBA Research Report, 21, London.

Higham, N. (1991a) 'Old light on the dark-age landscape: the description of Britain in the *De Excidio Britanniae* of Gildas', *Journal of Historical Geography*, forthcoming.

Higham, N. (1991b) 'Settlement, land-use and Domesday ploughlands', *Landscape History*, **12**, 33–44.

Hill, D. (1969) 'The burghal hidage: the establishment of a text', *Medieval Archaeology*, **13**, 84–92.

Hill, D. (1978) *Ethelred the Unready*, BAR, British Series, 59, Oxford.

Bibliography

Hill, D. (1981) *An Atlas of Anglo-Saxon England*, Oxford.

Hillam, J., Groves, C. M., Brown, D. M., Bailie, M. G. L., Coles, J. M. & Coles, B. J. (1990) 'Dendrochonology of the English Neolithic', *Antiquity*, **64**, 210–20.

Hingley, R. (1989) *Rural Settlement in Roman Britain*, London.

Hinton, D. (1981) 'Hampshire's Anglo-Saxon origins', in *The Archaeology of Hampshire*, ed. T. Shennan and R. T. Schadla Hall, London.

Hodder, I. (1979) 'Pre-Roman and Roman tribal economies', in *Invasion and Response: The Case of Roman Britain*, ed. B. Burnham and H. Johnson, BAR, British Series, 73, Oxford.

Hodges, R. (1982) *Dark Age Economics: The Origins of Towns and Trade AD 600–1000*, London.

Hodges, R. & Moreland, J. (1988) 'Power and exchange in Middle Saxon England', in *Power and Politics in Early Medieval Britain and Ireland*, ed. S. T. Driscoll and M. N. Nieke, Edinburgh.

Hodges, R. & Whitehouse, D. (1983) *Mohammed, Charlemagne and the Origins of Europe*, London.

Holmes, T. S. (ed.) (1896) *The Register of Ralph of Shrewsbury, Bishop of Bath and Wells, 1329–1363*, Somerset Record Society, Vols 9–10, Taunton.

Holt, J. C. (1982) 'Feudal society and the family in early medieval England: 1. The revolution of 1066', *TRHS*, **32**.

Hooke, D. (1981) *Anglo-Saxon Landscapes of the West Midlands: The Charter Evidence*, BAR, British Series, 95, Oxford.

Hooke, D. (1989) 'Early medieval estate and settlement patterns', in *The Rural Settlements of Medieval England*, ed. Aston, Austin and Dyer, Oxford.

Howlett, R. (1886) *Chronicles of the Reigns of Stephen, Henry II and Richard I, Vol. 1 (Gesta Stephani)*, London.

Hunt, T. S. (ed.) (1962) *The Medieval Customs of the Manors of Taunton and Bradford on Tone*, Somerset Record Society, Vol. 66, Taunton.

Johnson, S. (1975) 'Vici in lowland Britain', in *Small Towns of Roman Britain*, ed. W. Rodwell and T. Rowley, BAR, British Series, 15, Oxford.

Jones, B. & Mattingly, D. (1990) *An Atlas of Roman Britain*, Oxford.

Jones, G. R. J. (1979) 'Multiple estates and early settlement', in *English Medieval Settlement*, ed. P. H. Sawyer, London.

Keynes, S. (1980) *The Diplomas of King Æthelred 'the Unready' 978–1016*, Cambridge.

Keynes, S. & Lapidge, M. (eds) (1983) *Alfred the Great: Asser's Life of Alfred and Other Contemporary Sources*, London.

Kidd, A. (1989) *Eckweek in Wellow: A Case Study in the Organisation and Origins of the Medieval Landscape and Society of Somerset*, Bristol.

Knowles, D. (1963) *The Monastic Order in England: A History of its Development from the Times of St Dunstan to the Fourth Lateran Council, 940–1216*, 2nd ed., Cambridge.

Kurath, H. & Kuhn, S. (1952-) *A Middle English Dictionary*, Michigan.
Langmaid, N. (1971) 'Norton Fitzwarren', *Current Archaeology*, **28**, 116–20.
Lapidge, M. (1984) 'Gildas's education', in *Gildas: New Approaches*, ed. M. Lapidge and D. Dumville, Woodbridge.
Lapidge, M. & Herren, M. (eds) (1979) *Aldhelm, The Prose Works*, Ipswich.
Leach, P. J. (1982) *Ilchester, Vol. 1. Excavations 1974–5*, Bristol.
Leech, R. H. (1977) 'Romano-British rural settlement in south Somerset and north Dorset', unpublished Ph.D. thesis, University of Bristol.
Leech, R. H. (1980) 'Religion and burials in south Somerset and north Dorset', in *Temples, Churches and Religion in Roman Britain*, ed. W. Rodwell, Oxford.
Leech, R. H. (1982) 'The Roman interlude in the south-west: the dynamics of economic and social change in the Romano-British south Dorset and north Dorset', in *The Romano-British Countryside: Studies in Rural Settlement and Economy*, ed. D. Miles, BAR, British Series, 103, Oxford.
Leech, R. & Leach, P. (1982) 'Roman town and countryside 43-450 AD', in *The Archaeology of Somerset: A Review to 1500 AD*, ed. Aston and Burrow, Taunton.
Liddell, D. M. (1935) 'Report on the excavations at Hembury Fort, Devon', *PDAES*, **1**, 1–24.
Lowe, B. J. *et al.* (1987) 'Keynsham Abbey: excavations 1961–1985', *PSANHS*, **131**, 81–156.
Loyn, H. R. (1984) *The Governance of Anglo-Saxon England 500–1087*, London.
McDonald, J. & Snooks, G. D. (1986) *Domesday Economy: A New Approach to Anglo-Norman History*, Oxford.
McKitterick, R. (1983) *The Frankish Kingdoms under the Carolingians*, Harlow.
Manning, W. H. (1976) 'The conquest of the west country', in *The Roman West Country*, ed. K. Branigan and P. J. Fowler, Newton Abbot.
Margery, I. D. (1967) *Roman Roads of Britain*, 2nd ed., London.
Maxwell-Lyte, H. C. & Dawes, M. C. R. (eds) (1934 & 1935) *The Register of Thomas Bekynton*, Somerset Record Society, Vol. 49, parts i and ii, Taunton.
Meaney, A. (1964) *A Gazetteer of Early Anglo-Saxon Burials*, London.
Mercer, R. J. (1985) 'A Neolithic fortress and funeral center', *Scientific American*, **3**, 76–83.
Metcalf, D. M. (1978) 'The ranking of boroughs: numismatic evidence from the reign of Æthelred II', in *Ethelred the Unready*, ed. D. Hill, Oxford.
Metcalf, D. M. (1982) 'Anglo-Saxon coins 2: Alfred to Edgar', in *The Anglo-Saxons*, ed. J. Campbell, E. John and P. Wormald, Oxford.
Miller, M. (1976) 'Relative and absolute publication dates of Gildas's

De Excidio in medieval scholarship', *Bulletin of the Board of Celtic Studies*, **16**, 169–74.

Millett, M. (1990) *The Romanization of Britain*, Cambridge.

Minnit, S. (1974) 'An early Bronze Age hoard from Milverton, Somerset', *PSANHS*, **118**, 51–2.

Minnit, S. (1982) 'Farmers and field monuments 4000–2000 BC', in *The Archaeology of Somerset: A Review to 1500 AD*, ed. Aston and Burrow, Taunton.

Morgan, R. (1977) 'Tree ring studies in the Somerset Levels: the drove site of the Sweet Track', in *Somerset Levels Papers, 5*, ed. J. M. Coles, Cambridge.

Morris, J. (1973) *The Age of Arthur*, London.

Morris, R. (1983) *The Church in British Archaeology*, CBA Research Report, 47, London.

Musgrave, W. (1698) *The Philosophical Transactions of the Royal Society, No. 247.*

Page, W. (1911) *A History of the County of Somerset, Vol. 2*, London.

Peacock, D. P. S. (1969) 'A contribution to the study of Glastonbury ware from south-western Britain', *Antiquaries Journal*, **49**, 41–61.

Pearce, S. M. (1973) 'The dating of some Celtic dedications and the hagiographical traditions of south western Britain', *The Devonshire Association Report and Transactions*, **105**, 95–120.

Pearce, S. M. (1985) 'The early church in the landscape: the evidence from North Devon', *Archaeological Journal*, **142**, 255–75.

Poole, A. L. (1955) *Domesday Book to Magna Carta, 1087–1216*, 2nd ed., Oxford.

Porter, H. M. (1974–79) *S & DN & Q*, **30**, 71.

Rackham, O. (1977) 'Neolithic woodland management in the Somerset Levels: Garvins, Walton Heath and Rowland's Tracks', in *Somerset Levels Papers, 5*, ed. J. M. Coles, Cambridge.

Rackham, O. (1980) *Ancient Woodland: Its History, Vegetation and Uses in England*, London.

Radford, C. A. R. (1975) *Arthurian Sites in the West*, Exeter.

Radford, C. A. R. (1981) 'Glastonbury Abbey before 1184: interim report on the excavations, 1908–64', in *British Archaeological Association: Conference Transactions for the Year 1978*, Leeds.

Rahtz, P. (1951) 'The Roman temple at Pagan's Hill, Chew Stoke, North Somerset', *PSANHS*, **96**, 112–42.

Rahtz, P. (1969) 'Cannington Hillfort 1963', *PSANHS*, **113**, 53–64.

Rahtz, P. (1971) 'Excavations on Glastonbury Tor, Somerset, 1964–6', *Archaeological Journal*, **127**, 1–81.

Rahtz, P. (1977) 'Late Roman cemeteries and beyond', in *Burial in the Roman World*, ed. R. Reece, CBA Research Report, 22, London.

Rahtz, P. (1979) *The Saxon and Medieval Palaces at Cheddar*, BAR, British Series, 65, Oxford.

Rahtz, P. (1982) 'The Dark Ages, 400–700 A.D.' in *The Archaeology of Somerset: A Review to 1500 AD*, ed. Aston and Burrow, Taunton.

Rahtz, P. (1983) 'Celtic society in Somerset AD 400–700 The O'Donnell Lecture 1981', *Bulletin of the Board of Celtic Studies*, **30**, 174–200.

Rahtz, P. (1987) 'Post-Roman Avon', in *The Archaeology of Avon*, ed. Aston and Iles, Bristol.

Rahtz, P. & Greenfield, E. (1977) *Excavations at Chew Valley Lake, Somerset*, London.

Rahtz, P. & Harris, L. G. (1958) 'The temple well and other buildings at Pagan's Hill, Chew Stoke, North Somerset', *PSANHS*, **101**, 15–32.

Rahtz, P. & Hirst, S. M. (1974) *Beckery Chapel, Glastonbury 1967–8*, Glastonbury.

Renfrew, C. (1984) 'Monuments, mobilisation and social organisation in Neolithic Wessex', in *Approaches to Social Archaeology*, ed. Renfrew, Edinburgh.

Renn, D. (1973) *Norman Castles in Britain*, London.

Rivet, A. L. F. (1988) *Gallia Narbonensis*, London.

Rivet, A. L. F. & Smith, C. (1979) *The Place-Names of Roman Britain*, London.

Robinson, J. A. (1919) *The Saxon Bishops of Wells*, London.

Robinson, J. A. (1923) *The Times of St Dunstan*, Oxford.

Rodwell, W. (1980) *Temples, Churches and Religion in Roman Britain*, BAR, British Series, 77 (i), Oxford.

Rodwell, W. (1982) 'From mausoleum to minster: the early development of Wells Cathedral, in *The Early Church in Western Britain and Ireland*, ed. S. M. Pearce, BAR, British Series, 102, Oxford.

Rollason, D. (1989) *Saints and Relics in Anglo-Saxon England*, Oxford.

Ross, A. (1967) *Pagan Celtic Britain*, London.

Rowley, T. (ed.) (1981) *The Origins of Open-Field Agriculture*, London.

Rowley, T. (1983) *The Norman Heritage 1055–1200*, London.

Salway, P. (1981) *Roman Britain*, Oxford.

Scott, J. (1981) *The Early History of Glastonbury Abbey: An Edition, Translation and Study of William of Malmesbury's De Antiquitate Glastonie Ecclesie*, Woodbridge.

Smith, A. A. (ed.) (1970) *English Place-Name Elements*, English Place Name Society, Vols XXV and XVI, Cambridge.

Somerset Record Society 8, 'Members of the Society' (eds) (1894) *Two Cartularies of the Augustinian Priory of Bruton and the Cluniac Priory of Montacute in the County of Somerset*, Taunton.

Stafford, P. (1989) *Unification and Conquest: A Political and Social History of England in the Tenth and Eleventh Centuries*, London.

Stancliffe, C. (1983) 'Kings who opted out', in *Ideal and Reality in Frankish and Anglo-Saxon Society*, ed. P. Wormald, Oxford.

Stenton, F. M. (1947) *Anglo-Saxon England*, 2nd ed., Oxford.

Stevens, C. E. (1941) 'Gildas sapiens', *EHR*, **56**, 353–73.

Stone, J. F. & Wicks, A. T. (1935) 'Trial excavations at Hayes Wood Enclosure, Freshford, Somerset', *PSANHS*, **81**, 133–48.

Stubbs W. (ed.) (1874) *Memorials of St Dunstan*, Roll Series, 123, London.

Symons, T. (ed. and trans.) (1953) *Regularis concordia anglicae nationis monachorom sanctimonialiumque*, London.

Thomas, C. (1981) *Christianity and Roman Britain to AD 500*, London.

Thompson, E. A. (1984) *St Germanus of Auxerre and the End of Roman Britain*, Woodbridge.

Thorn, C. & Thorn, F. (eds and trans.) (1980) *The Domesday Book: Somerset*, Chichester.

Thorpe, B. (1868) *Analecta Anglo-Saxonica*, London.

Todd, S. (1984) 'Excavations at Hembury, Devon, 1980–3: a summary report', *Antiquaries Journal*, **64**, 251–68.

Wacher, J. (1974) *The Towns of Roman Britain*, London.

Wait, G. A. (1985) *Ritual and Religion in Iron Age Britain*, BAR, British Series, 149, Oxford.

Webster, G. (1980) *The Roman Invasion of Britain*, London.

Wedlake, W. J. (1958) *Excavations at Camerton, Somerset*, Bath.

Whitelock, D. (ed.) (1930) *Anglo-Saxon Wills*, Cambridge.

Whitelock, D. (1979a) 'A compilation on status', in *English Historical Documents, I, c. 500–1042*, 2nd ed., London.

Whitelock, D. (ed.) (1979b) *English Historical Documents, I, c. 500–1042*, 2nd ed., London.

Williams, M. (1970) *The Draining of the Somerset Levels*, Cambridge.

Winterbottom, M. (1977) 'Aldhelm's prose style and its origins', *Anglo-Saxon England*, **6**, 39–76.

Winterbottom, M. (ed.) (1978) *Gildas: The Ruin of Britain and Other Works*, Chichester.

Wormald, P. (1982) 'The ninth century', in *The Anglo-Saxons*, ed. Campbell, John and Wormald, Oxford.

Yorke, B. (1989) 'The Jutes of Hampshire and Wight and the origins of Wessex', in *The Origins of the Anglo-Saxon Kingdoms*, ed. S. Basset, Leicester.

Index